Southern Fiddlers and Fiddle Contests

Southern Fiddlers
and Fiddle Contests

Chris Goertzen

University Press of Mississippi

Jackson

www.upress.state.ms.us

The University Press of Mississippi is a member of
the Association of American University Presses.

Photographs by Chris Goertzen

Copyright © 2008 by University Press of Mississippi
All rights reserved
Manufactured in the United States of America

First printing 2008
∞
Library of Congress Cataloging-in-Publication Data

Goertzen, Chris.
Southern fiddlers and fiddle contests / Chris Goertzen.
p. cm. — (American made music series)
Includes bibliographical references and index.
ISBN 978-1-60473-122-4 (cloth : alk. paper) 1. Fiddlers—Southern
States. 2. Music—Competitions—Southern States. 3. Fiddling—Southern
States—History and criticism. I. Title.
ML3551.7.S68G64 2008
787.2079'75—dc22   2008015105

British Library Cataloging-in-Publication Data available

Contents

Preface

When I was an undergraduate at Austin College in Sherman, Texas, I sometimes carried a medium-sized black instrument case between my home and the downtown music store where I taught guitar and other stringed instruments. Once in a while, a resident of Sherman would ask: "Hey, whatcha got in there, a violin or a fiddle?" Sentence rhythm and body language told an interesting tale. The word "violin" was hurried through, uninflected, but "fiddle" got a little extra punch both in accent and volume, and the questioner's head would tilt a little, an eyebrow would lift, and a friendly smile would materialize. Nevertheless, I took the question literally the first few times, answering that what I was carrying was actually a viola, that it was a little bigger than a violin, that it was tuned a fifth lower, and . . . By this time, the questioner would nod in a way that both respected my eager explanation and urged me to finish. It was nice that I knew this stuff and was willing to pass it on, but a better answer would have been "fiddle."

In those years—the early 1970s—the relationship between town and gown was strained, since the average resident of Sherman and more than a few students at the college were far apart in attitudes toward the waning war in Vietnam. My being asked what instrument I was carrying was an expression of cautious friendliness, of seeking a bit of common ground, an elusive commodity then. We all liked music and knew that a violin and a fiddle looked the same. Did I play a violin, thus participating in an innocent aspect of the suspicious college scene? Or, even better, might my questioner and I have something in common, music that had been American for a long time and that you could enjoy—and perhaps play—no matter who you were and how little formal education you had endured? Did I fiddle or at least attend and enjoy fiddle contests?

Most academics who have turned their attention to American fiddling have been folklorists, though a few have been trained in ethnomusicology. Most of these scholars have concentrated on documenting the most venerable fiddlers and repertoires and on writing intimate histories of local traditions, paying attention to the present only as a window on what they consider to be a richer past. In contrast, this book deals with recent and current fiddling in a revival milieu that in many ways parallels contemporary folk institutions and festivals elsewhere in the industrialized West, particularly the transformed fiddle traditions of Canada, Ireland, Scotland, and Scandinavian countries. When I examine fiddling of the past in this book, it is mainly to understand the present better, though it is a present very much oriented toward the past.

Although my now quite ancient dissertation on fiddling deserves to rest undisturbed among legions of other dusty microforms, that work did launch me into fiddle research. I thank Bruno Nettl for giving me the freedom to bull ahead on this work in the first place and for his sound council during and long after my graduate school years. He is the once and future mentor. Larry Gushee first brought a fiddle commonplace book to my attention. Various archives of recordings, chief among these Indiana University's Archives of Traditional Music and the Library of Congress, helped me gather older performances of tunes. Travel in the summer of 2001 was supported by a University of Southern Mississippi Summer Research Grant. Thanks to my family for going to innumerable contests with me and for putting up with the mountains of paper that the work generated. Thanks to Paul Wells for his careful reading of and insightful recommendations for revision of the manuscript. And above all, thanks to all the fiddlers who have tolerated my curiosity over the decades. Though I am an academic with a primary audience of other academics, I hope that the fiddlers who were kind enough to help me learn about their craft and their lives will enjoy this book too.

This book is about fiddle contests, events lasting a weekend or a week, starring dozens of fiddlers whose innumerable individual performances of fiddle tunes last just a few minutes each. The core of the book approaches modern fiddle contests from complementary angles, looking in turn at the events as centered on the competition on stage (chapter 2), the festivals surrounding the competition (chapter 3), the fiddlers themselves (chapter 4), and the tunes and styles of modern fiddling (chapter 5). The first chapter presents a summary of what we can know for sure about the history of fiddling, with some emphasis on fiddle contests over past centuries. The end of chapter 5 concerns the history of fiddling as lived at contests: what fiddlers and audiences believe about fiddling as embodying history as it should have been. This is fiddling as nostalgia, fiddling that we can know something about but care about even more, the fiddling that will continue vigorously into the future while referring constantly to the past.

Southern Fiddlers and Fiddle Contests

CHAPTER ONE

American Fiddling of the Past

O nce a year, in the second-largest shopping mall in Tuscaloosa, Alabama, fiddlers and other musicians gather for a contest lasting from Friday evening through a long Saturday. There is a temporary stage set up at one end of McFarland Mall's food court for the competition, and each of the half-dozen seating areas built into the corridors also fill with people wielding fiddles, guitars, banjos, mandolins, basses, and even harmonicas. But the built-in benches don't suffice, so the musicians shape additional stations with their own folding chairs. The jamming and socializing are at least as important as the contest itself.

The music coming from the stage (and from all over the mall) centers on two-part dance tunes, especially rapid "breakdowns," many modern versions of

Figure 1. Roy Crawford and Cullman County Bluegrass competing in Tuscaloosa in 2004. The contest stage is at one end of the McFarland Mall food court.

eighteenth-century reels and hornpipes, and yet more younger compositions in the same vein. There are ragtime tunes too, and waltzes, and plenty of singing, often of songs dating from the 1920s and 1930s. Performers' skill levels vary wildly within each age group. Some kids are just sawing their way through "Bile Them Cabbage Down"; others seem to be coming along in the Suzuki approach to violin (but remain beginners as fiddlers); and a few show both talent and accomplishment as genuine contest-style fiddlers at remarkably young ages. The seniors vary dramatically in skill too: some only close friends and immediate family can bear to listen to, while a few others are fluent in various styles of fiddling—bluegrass, Texas-style contest fiddling, or old-time—or are quite idiosyncratic. Then, in the middle range by age (that is, between seventeen and sixty), the range of skill rises and narrows: even the weakest players are fairly fluent, and the strongest are stunningly virtuosic.

Most participants in the Tuscaloosa contest (both the performers and the many audience members who came to the mall for this purpose) are dressed neatly but informally, and most behave like old friends at a neighborhood barbecue or a family reunion. The amplification system is adjusted to a volume that suits both listening and socializing: you can hear the music well even if your neighbors are chatting, and if you choose to converse, you don't have to yell. In fact, no one listens closely to the whole event, although each member of the audience pays careful attention now and again. A given individual may focus on the stage when a performance stands out in terms of quality, and again when a friend or family member is playing, and perhaps also during, for example, the harmonica competition if the individual plays that instrument. In addition, audience members tune in *some* of the time just because they feel they ought to. This event is not just fun: there is an underlying and pervasive feeling that these tunes are old, real American music. Showing respect for this music and the people that make an effort to play it well shows respect for a way of life, for America as it used to be in the good old days. Or for how the good old days should have been, anyway.

From Late-Eighteenth-Century Scotland to Mid-Twentieth-Century America

A country that has never held still—one with a history of immigration and frequent relocation—needs symbolic anchors, reminders of the past that aren't just pictures on the wall or tales in books but that are celebrated through actions. Indeed, the speed with which the United States was settled—and the rapid transformation from a nation of immigrants to a population deeply, often defensively,

American, and still on the move—has produced a national psychology rife with dovetailing conflicts. Formal education is respected but sometimes perceived as sabotaging effectiveness in daily tasks; homespun horse sense is more reliable. And however self-confident we as a nation are in facing practical tasks, we have long leaned on Europe for a variety of cultural models, looking particularly to Great Britain, unsurprisingly.

In short, the facts of a young country and rapid, inescapable change spawned a powerful inner need for embodiments of a usable past with British connections. Americans have had to believe that change is healthy, but maintaining a national habit of boldly seeking one physical or mental frontier after another has been psychologically sustainable only because it has been balanced by profound feelings of nostalgia. Fiddling has a place in this picture because it's a way to celebrate down-home fun, competence, and historically grounded cultural patriotism at the same time. A good fiddler is self-reliant, hard-working, full of humor, and skilled in an impressive but not intimidating way. And fiddling helps maintain that channel through American culture that refers back to Europe, and specifically Great Britain, with respect and energy but without any taint of *Masterpiece Theatre* snobbery.

How did we get from Britain of the distant past to a modern fiddle contest in Tuscaloosa, Alabama? Many of the fiddle tunes heard today have been American for centuries, but a fair number of those venerable tunes were British before that, with well-documented histories reaching back well into the eighteenth century in Britain, specifically Scotland. These include, among many other such tunes, "Leather Britches" (called "Lord McDonald's Reel" in eighteenth-century Scotland), "Billy in the Low Grounds" (formerly "The Braes of Auchtertyre" in Scotland), and "Turkey in the Straw" (originally "Rose Tree" in England, though passing through the minstrel tune "Zip Coon" on the way to the current title). These melodies, the dance types to which they belong, and the social situations in which they flourished define the roots of American fiddling.

The earliest British settlers in the future United States had little time to relax. Nevertheless, a Virginia statute of 1618 forbade Sabbath-day "dancing, fiddling, card-playing, hunting, and fishing," so there must have been some interest in each of these pursuits (Dulles 1965, 8). The progressively more tolerant behavioral standards of the colonies in the eighteenth century were illustrated by an increase in evidence of fiddling. We know little about which tunes American fiddlers played before the Revolutionary War, but the 1790s through the first two decades of the nineteenth century became a heyday of fiddle tunes both in the countryside and in fashionable urban American musical life. This is a well-documented era, in part owing to the antiquarian bent of many past students of American music and of libraries. "American" fiddle tunes of that time were still mostly English, including, of course, the countless Scottish tunes then popular in England (see Goertzen 1982). Then, fashion changed and the dance types and the songs connected with fiddling were pushed out of the urban mainstream into pockets in the countryside, surviving best in the South. The publication of fiddle tunes (mostly in the North!) continued throughout the nineteenth century, but the evidence thus provided is progressively sparser and less detailed. The best evidence concerning fiddling outside of the Northeast comes from just two rare southern publications, Knauff's *Virginia Reels* (1839) and Person's *Popular Airs* (1889), both of which illustrate how fiddling still looked back to the British Isles (especially Scotland) but also was integral to a specifically American entertainment, blackface minstrelsy.

Much of the history of nineteenth-century America concerns massive population movement and connected cultural change. Individuals, families, even major parts of communities moved west, often skipping the middle of the country, with later generations eventually filling in that gap. Regional fiddle styles coalesced in the Southeast, and fiddlers were among the thousands of restless citizens packing up and leaving home for areas where people were fewer, land cheap, and opportunities in general greater. Most who headed west did so for reasons fundamentally different from those that inspired the Pilgrims and Puritans to cross the Atlantic. While the movement west also included groups emigrating partly for religious reasons—for example, the Quakers' move from North Carolina to Indiana, and the Mormons' trek to Utah—most were sacrificing the cultural richness of settled communities for economic opportunity. As settlers moved west across the South, fiddling came along with them. Marcus Bailey recounted how the family of his great-grandfather traveled from Kentucky to Alabama in 1814, meeting the Acton family of Tennessee inside the Alabama border. "There were fiddles and good fiddlers in both families. I might be safe in saying that one of the first fiddling sessions in the state of Alabama was held on the banks of the Tennessee River" that night (1983, 21).

We know much more about an immigrant to Texas who was a fiddler, simply because this rough-hewn and loquacious polymath, Gideon Lincecum (1793–1874), left behind a handful of narratives about fiddling, one describing a serendipitous picnic in 1835 near Eagle Lake, about thirty miles west of Houston. Gideon, then residing in Missouri, had brought a few neighbors to see if Texas would be a suitable place to relocate. On the day of this particular picnic, Gideon was traveling alone. A Mr. Heard, with whom Gideon had recently stayed, happened along with two neighbor families. This group had a picnic planned. Gideon joined forces with them and invited the families to camp overnight with him. I quote:

The carriages were immediately unloaded, and the negroes started back for a supply of blankets, more bread, coffee and so on. One of the younger men told the negro to bring his violin,—which was as much as to say invite the neighborhood to come.

[More settlers and Indian acquaintances Gideon had made that day assembled gradually.]

Seeing the violin case thrown out amongst their pots and blankets, and not having had one in my hands for months, I was hungry for music. I opened the case and found a splendid violin, in excellent condition. I took it out, and going near to two or three ladies, said, "some of you were telling a new comer what the wild man could do. With this good violin, I will furnish you with a little story that will bear telling as long as you live." I performed "Washington's Grand March" so loud that I could distinctly hear the tune repeated as it returned from the echo on the opposite lake shore. I could feel that my very soul mingled with the sound of the instrument, and, at the time I was about to become so entranced as to be unfit for such jovial company; the handsome lady ran up and, slapping me on the shoulder, exclaimed, "Good heavens, Doctor! Where are you going?" I was startled, and training [tuning?] up the violin, performed Gen. Harrison's march, then Hail Columbia and then the No. 1 cotillion in the beggar set". They all went to dancing . . .

Everything being in readiness Mrs. Heard beat a tumbler with the handle of a knife, and the fiesta commenced. They ate, and bragged, and laughed, until the darkness came, and they had waked all the echoes of the old lake. Then they called up the Negro fiddler and tried to dance awhile, but the grass was too much for them; when one of the ladies proposed that all should be seated and get the Doctor to treat them to a few pieces of his good music . . . (1874, 10–12).

The African American who fiddled at this picnic may stand for hundreds of slave fiddlers busy at white dances (see, for example, Stoutamire 1972, 27–32). Such occasions constituted the real beginning of the black-white musical interchange that would be so important for American music in general (and specifically for fiddling). Blacks played white dance tunes, but just what liberties did they take with these melodies, accidentally or not? When blackface minstrelsy (which would become the most popular stage entertainment of mid-nineteenth-century America) boomed starting in 1843, the genre's white male quartets claimed they were imitating blacks. Most of the blacks these showmen had heard making music were likely slave fiddlers. These blacks may well have expressed their African heritage by favoring the British tunes that were rhythmically relatively complex—thus, Scottish tunes—and then taking additional rhythmic freedoms with these melodies. It is

true that some of the early published music of minstrelsy is extremely simple, por-
traying blacks as childlike, but more is mildly exotic, and in fact often Scottish
in origin (see Goertzen and Jabbour 1987 and Goertzen 1991). We can follow the
black-white musical interchange a few more steps. After the Civil War, African
American blackface troupes began to appear. To earn a living, they had to please
white audiences and thus had to imitate the skits and the musical performances of
the established white troupes. Late in the century, minstrelsy expanded—and eventually dissolved into variety and vaudeville—but survived in its old-fashioned form
in the medicine show. Performers such as country music star Roy Acuff learned
from both black and white medicine show fiddlers and banjoists. In sum, by the
time we get to Acuff's generation, we have white medicine show performers learning from black blackface minstrels who copied the whites who had imitated black
slave fiddlers who had been trained to play white dance tunes. Could musical interaction and synthesis have been avoided? That both Gideon Lincecum and slaves
fiddled at that 1835 picnic in frontier Texas was nothing unusual, just a tiny illustration of the black-white musical interchange so important for American music.

As the nineteenth century progressed, publishing became increasingly mono-
lithic. The large publishing houses centered in major cities influenced the output
of small-scale publishers more and more, and the vagaries of fashion turned further
and further away from fiddle tunes. Though these continued to be printed in significant numbers, they received little editorial attention. Nevertheless, many tunes
likely remained in oral tradition at this time. Toward mid-century, publisher Elias
Howe nearly cornered the market for anthologies of miscellaneous instrumental
music. His collections, and the expansions of these later in the century by William
Ryan, Septimus Winner, and the firm of Carl Fischer, dominated fiddle tune publication. Of the forty or so fiddle tunes that continued to be published frequently
through the nineteenth century, a fair number remain well-known today, including
"College Hornpipe" (now often called "Sailor's Hornpipe," theme of the Popeye
cartoons), "Devil's Dream," "Durang's Hornpipe," "Fisher's Hornpipe," "Flowers of
Edinburgh," "Liverpool Hornpipe," "McDonald's Reel" (now "Leather Britches"
in the South), "Miss Brown's Reel" (now "Wagoner" or "Tennessee Wagoner"),
"Money Musk" (a northern tune today), "Old Zip Coon" (now "Turkey in the
Straw"), "Rickett's Hornpipe" (northern today), and "Soldier's Joy." Indeed, several of the tunes Gideon Lincecum played at the 1835 picnic in Texas were and
remained common in such anthologies.

A resurgence of interest in fiddling during the 1920s was less a genuine revival
than a moment of bold punctuation marking the completion of the shift of fiddling from the center of musical life to the lively but smallish subculture of today.
The nineteenth-century publication of fiddle tunes by Howe, Winner, Ryan, and

others was extended by Pepper (1896 and reprints) and others, and eventually by Cole (*One Thousand Fiddle Tunes* 1940, reprinted many times). But when commercial recording of fiddling blossomed briefly in the 1920s, most of what southern fiddlers played had little to do with those publications, which turned out to represent significant fractions of active repertoires only in a few large cities and in New England. We can, however, generalize about the average fiddlers' activities by conflating published accounts. He (almost always "he") played at all kinds of secular gatherings in rural areas, including "country socials, picnics, county fairs, country dances, and fiddlers' conventions" (Young 1971, 31). Though almost never a full-time professional musician, he frequently was paid something for his efforts (Koon 1969, 56). He might play alone, or with other fiddlers, guitarists, banjoists, keyboard players (especially of the reed organ), and so forth (Randolph 1932, 69; Bronner 1977, 63; and Wilgus 1971, 43). Though he often picked up much of his repertoire from older male relatives who fiddled, tunes also were spread by fiddlers who entertained themselves while traveling on business (Graham 1951, 71) or who themselves undertook long journeys specifically for the purpose of learning new tunes (Randolph 1932, 71). He might even have read music in a laborious fashion (Guthrie 1972, 52, and others). And this profile would hold well into the century for plenty of older fiddlers, as is demonstrated in the fiddlers' biographies assembled to accompany the best of many adamantly retrospective published tune collections, those by Bayard (1944 and 1982) and Titon (2001).

Of the wide assortment of performance forums available to the early-twentieth-century fiddler, the contest or convention was the only one based on listening passively to tunes. The series of early-twentieth-century contests most widely celebrated in print was that based in Atlanta, Georgia, though contests also took place at about the same time along the Mississippi (Graham 1951, 71), in Kentucky (Combs 1960, 116), and in upper middle Tennessee, this last sponsored by the Daughters of the Confederacy, a retrospective link common for contests in that area (Wolfe 1980, 50–52). The well-publicized series of annual contests in Atlanta was sponsored by the Georgia Old Time Fiddlers Association and lasted from 1913 to 1935. This may have been the first so regular a succession of contests (Daniel 1980, 67). And this was the first substantial formal organization to promote fiddling systematically; such associations would become critical in the maintenance of fiddle contests in the 1950s and 1960s.

Even during the first few years of the Atlanta contests, these events were large for the time, attracting twenty-five to seventy-five contestants, most from within an eighty-mile radius of Atlanta (Meade 1969, 27), and an audience that grew to more than four hundred. Older fiddlers generally won. In fact, the champion was often John Carson or Gid Tanner, both of whom would become famous as recording artists in the 1920s. The judges at these contests must have valued showmanship more than refined musicianship for these two mediocre fiddlers to have triumphed so regularly (Cohen 1975, 119). One critic in 1914 stated that "a more nondescript collection of people had never been grouped together on a single stage in Atlanta," and then described the repertoire in summary fashion: "such tunes as "Old Zip Coon," "Billy in the Low Ground," "Katie Hill," "Soapsuds over the Fence" and "Moonshine Bob" fairly poured from the fiddlers" (see Meade 1969, 29).

The 1920 incarnation of the Atlanta contest attracted plenty of attention from Atlanta newspapers. Wayne Daniel collated these reports, and I shall draw primarily on his article on them (1980) for the following paragraphs. He found that the reporters described the fiddlers, their instruments, their repertoires, and the audience all as old and mossy but nevertheless quite vital in the countryside. The audience included plenty of folks who, regardless of their station in society, clearly knew and loved fiddling. "Many an Atlanta banker and businessman would rather lose an arm than miss a [fiddlers'] convention," quoted Daniel. Whether or not these upper-crust citizens were city-bred, much of the populace of Atlanta consisted of recent immigrants from the countryside, people who had heard fiddling regularly during their childhoods. The audience encompassed all generations. A Saturday afternoon performance was scheduled so that "grandpa and grandma and the children" could "hear the fiddlers without exposure to the night air" (69).

Portrayals of the fiddlers emphasized their advanced ages and rustic eccentricity. We can assume that this emphasis was chosen partly to make good stories, but even if these were caricatures, there was plenty of fodder for them. These men were "mountaineers and swamp dwellers who made and consumed large quantities of moonshine 'likker,' fiddled and danced at square dances every Saturday night of the year, and sometimes farmed on the side" (67). One Uncle Bud Littlefield, "whose countenance was adorned with 'two feet of white whiskers,' informed his listeners that up where he came from 'we raise corn, hell and fiddlers, and we had a pretty good crop this year, all around'" (71). Another contestant was "an 85-year-old veteran who rattled the bones in a way to make a minstrel end-man envious" (72).

The physical fiddles played at the contest also received considerable comment. The instrument played by one Jim Goolsby was "a fiddle such as Kriesler never saw and Kubelik never dreamed of touching. It was built by his own hands from a cigar box, a hoe handle and assorted sizes of wire strings, and when tickled with a bow made of half a barrel hoop and well-rosined horsehair" made "sounds guaranteed to make a $90 saxaphone [sic] in a jazz band sob with envy" (71). Another instrument, after having been employed to jack up a Ford, had been repaired by the judicious application of tobacco juice. In any case, fiddles were considered as distinct from and morally superior to violins: "a violinist plays by note and a fiddler by plain natural disposition and elbow grease; . . . a violinist draws down about a thousand a night, a week, a month or whatever it is, if it's so, the fiddler is lucky to get the neck of the chicken and what's left in the bottle after it's done been 'round the room," said one Judge Jackson (72).

Although several of the contestants often presented fiddle tunes within skits recalling blackface minstrelsy, among them famous fiddlers such as perennial champion Fiddlin' John Carson and Gid Tanner (Burrison 1977, 73, 80), this was just part of the picture. On the other end of a spectrum of relative propriety, the winner of the 1920 contest played only religious tunes (Daniel 1980, 72). Overall, the rampant rusticity wasn't actively depraved but rather harmlessly frisky. Supposed hell-raising was portrayed by the press through the rosy lens of nostalgia.

While the Atlanta contests present a fascinating mix of the vitality of the country/city continuum with an admixture of nostalgia, another set of contests tilted more in the direction of pure nostalgia, being primarily symbolic. Rich automaker Henry Ford connected what he believed to be a pernicious eroding of moral standards by the 1920s with prevailing musical taste and so financed an extensive series of fiddle contests and square dances at Ford dealerships in order to offer an alternative to modern foolishness. A *Literary Digest* article from 1926 entitled "Fiddling to Henry Ford" chimed in with Ford's sentiments while reporting on this series of contests. The anonymous author decried the "synthetic music of Tin Pan Alley" and its link with "the promiscuous methods adopted for public dancing," which "drove tens of thousands of mature dancers from the floor" (33). And Maine fiddler Mellie Dunham, the best-known of the many fiddlers Ford invited to visit him in Dearborn, Michigan, was critical of jazz (as was Ford himself): Jazz music, Dunham said, "has no rhythm and melody to my way of thinking. Perhaps they're all right, but I don't think much of these modern dances. This jazzing is not so good for young people. It lets them loaf too much" (34).

In contrast to the claimed reprehensible qualities of most early-twentieth-century music and dance, fiddling and square dancing were portrayed in this article as "innocent and neighborly cavorting," as "large-hearted, social, and wholesome" in a manner reflecting "those whose characters and traditions shaped the nation" (33). And fiddler Mellie Dunham, "the seventy-two-year-old Pine Tree state farmer and snow-shoe maker," was a "simple country gentleman," an "old-fashioned fiddler," perhaps quaint, but certainly good-hearted and industrious (38).

Other remarks quoted in this article differentiate fiddling from violin playing, citing fiddlers' reliance on oral tradition and pan-generational appeal. Dunham said "No, I never took a lesson. I saw a picture once of Ole Bull, and I studied the way he held his violin. That's all I know about technique. I don't pretend to be a musician. I'm just a fiddler. Notes mean little or nothing to me. Everything I play, I've learned by hearin' others" (34). The article's author added that "the tunes that live in fiddles like Mr. Dunham's are fast dying out. Here and there they have been captured and put down so that they may live for future generations. Their origin is, more often than not, entirely unknown to the men who have played them count-less times; like Mellie, they have heard them on other fiddles and repeated them on their own. . . . These melodies were written to lure alike grandmother by the fireside and the girl not yet in her 'teens. If America has folk-songs they are to be found in these early and somewhat homely tunes created (one could scarcely say composed) for the fiddle" (36). But Ford's own affection for fiddling issued from his love of the wholesome and invigorating square dance, which, like the fiddling that accompanied it, was still a living tradition in the countryside, despite its being thought to be in danger of "dying out."

In a congruent development during the early 1920s, a number of southern radio stations began to broadcast live music by local performers. These performers were often already locally popular through their appearances at political gatherings near their homes. Malone notes that "in the commercial exploitation of Southern folk music the phonograph industry was only a step behind the broadcasting busi-ness" (1968, 37). The "hillbilly" recording artist was usually both singer and instru-mentalist. He remained a part-time musician for whom recording was primarily a means of self-advertisement rather than a source of significant income. Fiddle tunes formed a substantial part of the repertoires of many hillbilly artists. Their se-lections of tunes reflected rural repertoires, but these were not passive reflections. Many "folk" musicians learned tunes from records made by their modestly remu-nerated brethren. It was not a new or startling thing for fiddle tunes to flourish in the complex "symbiotic relationship between commercial and folk culture" (see Wilgus 1971, 172). But recordings contained more information about the music than prints of fiddle tunes could, and were popular in places minimally touched by publications.

It is difficult to assess precisely the impact of recorded hillbilly music, in part because most company files are no longer available and surviving industry person-nel either never knew or cannot recall marketing statistics. In a carefully researched and closely reasoned article concerning the Columbia 15000-D series of records, the famous 1920s series called "Familiar Tunes—Old and New," Charles Wolfe found that, from 1925 through 1931, traditional instrumental music (usually fid-dle tunes, with or without texts) comprised 10.5 percent of the titles issued and 12.2 percent of the items sold in this collection (1978, 120). Many such tunes were distributed in well over ten thousand copies. This series enjoyed nationwide distribution, though the emphasis in marketing for this and other companies was southern, often with specific recordings targeted on given areas. But this first decade of hillbilly recording antedated the dominance of star performers of country music, and Wolfe believes that many purchasers "bought the song rather than the singer" (1978, 125).

The breadth of public interest in fiddle tunes evidenced by purchases of recordings was retrospective and temporary. An article in *The Etude* of 1929 noted the return of the "country fiddler" in contests and in vaudeville and emphasized that old players were especially valued ("Aged Fiddlers" 1929, 133). Dr. Humphrey Bate, the first artist to popularize old-time music on the radio in Nashville, referred to fiddle tunes variously as "The Old Master's," "Old Time Fiddlin' Tunes," and "old favorites" (Wolfe 1977, 1–2). A number of collections of fiddle tunes drawing on active repertoires appeared around this time to tap a general market for things "old." And both the Atlanta fiddle contests and Henry Ford's efforts to oust what he saw as the immoralities associated with jazz through a return to square dancing and fiddling present those traditions as quaint and marginal, despite how valuable they were for a matrix of symbolic reasons. The Atlanta contests faded away in the 1930s, just as did fiddle contests throughout most of the United States. Many good fiddlers laid down their bows for a time, though enough did not that another revival would be possible a few decades later.

In the mid-1930s, the Library of Congress began to accumulate sizeable collections of field recordings of fiddle tunes, dovetailing with the slackening of recording of fiddle tunes by hillbilly artists and the temporary demise of the fiddle contest system. Collecting spread through the continental United States, emphasizing the rural South (see Jabbour 1977). Musical items deposited in the Library's Archive of Folk Song through July 1940 are indexed by title in an instructive checklist (1942). The most popular titles, most of which had some association with a text, include "Arkansas Traveller," "Buffalo Gals," "Cacklin' Hen" (various similar titles), "Cripple Creek," "Cumberland Gap," "Devil's Dream" (no text association), "Leather Britches" (rarely texted), "Mississippi Sawyer," "Old Joe Clark," "Sally Goodin," "Soldier's Joy," "Sourwood Mountain," and "Turkey in the Straw." In addition to "Billy in the Low Ground," somewhat less common fiddle tunes on this list include "Bonaparte's Retreat," "Eighth of January," "Fisher's Hornpipe," "Fox Chase," "Irish Washerwoman," and "Wagoner."

While the brief efflorescence of fiddling in the 1920s drew on a reasonably vital rural tradition, a somewhat parallel movement in the 1950s and 1960s was more of a genuine revival. A few contests bridged these eras, but changes in the mainstream of popular music—both in *what* was popular and *how* it was marketed—had almost completely squelched fiddling in most parts of the United

States. But, when most social functions that had once been home to fiddling no longer welcomed fiddlers regularly, the idea of the contest would bloom as the focus for a modest but enduring subculture. Contests such as the "convention" in Galax, Virginia, grew mightily during these years, and a contest that would become extremely influential started far away in Weiser, Idaho, in 1953. This event, modest in scope in its earliest years, grew steadily in size until it became the "national" contest. Today, most contests in the West and northern Midwest are modeled on the enormous contest in Weiser. Texas is, however, the source of the styles that dominate in that state and through much of the United States today. Southeastern fiddlers stick to forms of their inherited old-timey styles, other fiddlers espouse varieties of fiddling associated with bluegrass, but much of the country plays in "contest" style, actually a complex of listening-oriented melodically intricate styles based on the contest fiddling of Texas. The revival of fiddling in the areas drawing primarily on Texas style was fairly self-conscious and can be tracked over time easily. Fiddling in the old-timey areas also evolved over the decades. But all American fiddling joined in a general transformation from a weakened ingredient of mainstream culture to a vital subculture anchored by the fiddle contest.

Old, New, and Real: The Case of Mississippi's Senator George Cecil McLeod

Although fiddling as both music and as social practice changed dramatically during the twentieth century, the changes were gradual. The oldest fiddlers active both in the middle of the twentieth century and today have lived through these transformations, sometimes helping change come about, at other times resenting and resisting it. I will illustrate how fiddlers' lives and activities have changed in the last half-century through a case study of a fiddler who started fiddling in an environment firmly set in the past. He is George Cecil McLeod, a farmer and former Mississippi state senator.

Three McLeod brothers migrated from the Isle of Skye to North Carolina about 1800; then two of them relocated to Mississippi. George Cecil represents the fifth generation of McLeods in the state. His family background thus echoes several broad trends in southern demography and in the history of American fiddling. Many Scots immigrated to rural areas of the southern colonies and later southern United States, and so their musical taste strongly influenced the formation of composite southern musical taste. Their distinctive and rhythmically complex fiddling was especially apt for mixing with blacks' performance practices over the history of blackface minstrelsy in the South. Second, many southerners interested in traditional music issued from a broad trend in settlement in the South: families of southerners gradually spread west across the South (very quickly in the McLeod's case) and often have been in the South for generations. They identify themselves as southerners more than as members of any ethnic group.

McLeod was born in 1927, just outside of Leakesville, in the piney woods of southeast Mississippi. But any romantic equating of "rural" with "isolated" would be hasty and simplistic, even for the time when McLeod was a child. Workers in lumber camps moved regularly from logged-out areas to newer opportunities; one local logger and fiddler brought tunes from Canada home with him. Camp Shelby, southeast of Hattiesburg, housed military professionals and draftees from throughout the nation; a violin repairman of German extraction trained there during World War II. And the nearby Gulf Coast has always been cosmopolitan.

McLeod's father didn't fiddle, but fiddlers were far from hard to find. McLeod recalls that "a high percentage of the folks, either their Daddy, or their Granddaddy, or their Uncle, or their neighbor, played the fiddle. In their younger days, they would have gone visiting [to a fiddler's home], or they knew that their Daddy had, or their parents had . . . very few people hadn't been exposed to fiddling." This echoes another broad factor in the history of music in the rural South: fiddling remained more central in musical life here longer than elsewhere in the United States, for a mix of demographic and financial reasons.

Young George Cecil regularly sought out the company of the two most skilled fiddlers in the area, his uncle and especially a distant neighbor named Jode Denmark, who was born in 1891 into a family in which many of the men fiddled. I found this to be a common pattern among older fiddlers: they had more than one mentor close to home and knew fiddlers both within and outside of their family. McLeod's main teacher, Denmark, "had a little farm . . . maybe worked some turpentine and logged wood some. He repaired instruments a good bit." Even before he made many treks to hear Denmark play, McLeod was regularly exposed to fiddling: "Uncle M. L. Griffin, who married my Daddy's sister; they had eight children, all of them older than I was. They were all talented musically, and my uncle played the fiddle. And that's where the young folks up in Leakesville would gather up on Saturday night to dance. They'd clear the furniture out of one room and the hall, and Uncle M. L. would play, with some of the children accompanying him, some on guitar, and some of the girls would sometimes play piano [or] accordion. They danced in the bedroom and in the hall connecting."

Fiddlers back then typically started playing later in life than the best fiddlers of today. By the time McLeod finally owned a fiddle, his head was full of fiddle tunes. He was in the tenth grade. His school band director, a violinist, gave McLeod lessons for about six months until the director was drafted. When

McLeod finished high school, he attended Mississippi State University for a year, then went into the navy for sixteen months. He returned in the fall of 1946 and soon had a semester of violin lessons from the head of the music department at Mississippi State College for Women, about twenty miles east of Mississippi State University, where he was enrolled. He summarizes that he has "had a few violin lessons, but not enough to hurt [my] fiddling," a verbal formula common among fiddlers.

McLeod played a fiddle tune called "Sugar Foot Rag" on his first date with the woman he would marry. "When I met her, I had just learned it, and it was fresh on my mind. I heard that tune one night [on the radio], when I was out in the pickup. And it appealed to me. And I got to humming it. The next morning I got up, and while Mama was cooking breakfast I learned it. And it's always been one that I liked to play." This sort of learning process, that is, inexact replication in which a remembered outline is fleshed out anew by individuals who therefore had to command and exercise considerable creative ability, was more common then than now. In contrast, today's ubiquitous tape recorder allows fiddlers to emulate one another with as much precision as the learner's technical ability permits.

McLeod's hearing a fiddle tune on the radio in 1950 fit southern trends more than national ones. Indeed, fiddling was still part of local daily life during McLeod's young adulthood in the early 1950s. He performed at square dances and other functions all over the area. He had less time to fiddle in the early 1960s, coincidentally at the same time that fiddling was being pushed aside in popular consciousness. The biographical factor was simple: the McLeods had entered the dairy business, a grueling occupation leaving little time for recreation. The audience for fiddling was shrinking anyway, owing to the inroads of rock music among the young and a concerted effort by the media to make public entertainment more streamlined and thus profitable through economies of scale. But McLeod returned to fiddling. He described his performing hiatus as follows: "Through the '50s, I played right smart. I got in the dairy business in '61 . . . And I didn't play hardly any fiddle from the time I started dairying until I got into the campaign [for state senator] in '67. Consequently, I wasn't in real good playing form then, but then after I found out it worked in politics, I got a chance to go to more functions and have more reason to play some, I went back to playing some. And then we had the first bluegrass festival near Chatom [Alabama] here in '71. So from that point on, I began to hear fiddlers more."

Thus, the interval between decline and revival of fiddling in this part of the Deep South was remarkably brief, and not so very long ago. Indeed, when Mr. McLeod took up the fiddle again, some of the same forums for performance were there as earlier (though some of these have gradually declined since). The use of

fiddling at political rallies was one such forum: McLeod's opponents didn't spon-
sor fiddle music, but he offered it himself, with telling moments of hesitation:

> Even when I ran for office in '67 and through the '70s, especially in the early '70s, I
> hadn't even thought about the effect that the fiddle would have when I was campaign-
> ing, because it was just something I liked to do. . . . But when you're running, you go
> through the newspaper offices, radio stations, TV stations, and the local printer
> to print up stuff to advertise, to get people to remember you to vote for you. . . .
> I'd played in all these rural counties. I'd gone and played at the cakewalks, plays, PTA
> meetings, and dances, and at home. . . . Everybody knew I played the fiddle. [Before
> giving a speech, I'd] go and play the fiddle. . . . And the folks around here were say-
> ing; "Now, don't go and play that thing down in Jackson County [on the coast].
> Folks will ridicule you if you do." [But] folks in Jackson County was country folks
> [even if they had moved to the city]. So I carried my fiddle . . . I got up, introduced
> myself, and told them I wanted to play a little bit . . . and just slid on into the tune. I
> didn't play but just [a few moments] and there was a half a dozen couples up square
> dancing, and the crowd was clapping and keeping time for them before I quit the
> tune. . . . And the next week I was down there in Jackson County passing out cards,
> and I very seldom came across somebody that hadn't heard of some fellow that
> played the fiddle.

It is striking both that McLeod's constituents in rural Greene County thought
that the presumably more cosmopolitan residents of a county on the coast would
look down on fiddle music and that those constituents were at least temporarily
wrong. These residents of Greene County apparently were self-conscious about
their own enjoyment of a slice of culture that was explicitly old-fashioned by then,
though it had been right at the center of rural entertainment when many of them
were children. That McLeod's disagreement with their prediction of urban disdain
for fiddling was on target was owing to his keener sense of demography; however,
the difference in taste that they wrongly thought was in place around 1970 certainly has materialized since. I can't imagine fiddling being thought anything better than quaint at a political rally in Jackson County now. McLeod still plays at
rallies in Greene County occasionally, although he feels that the political rally as
an institution has declined considerably. After all, we no longer need to assemble
to learn what candidates think. But small traditional political rallies still occur in
Greene County, and organizers welcome McLeod's fiddling out of respect for him.
I attended one held June 13, 2003, on a farm in the county. My impression on arriving was of pickup truck after pickup truck, and of powerful odors of barbecue.
Local candidates spoke briefly, as did the Republican gubernatorial candidate in a

whirlwind stop. He shook all hands, praised George Cecil's fiddling, gave a quick speech in which recollections of hunting segued into references to Greene County and then to promises concerning tort reform and other themes certain to reso- nate, and was gone. Had he heard the fiddling? Had anyone? The fact that it was Republican stalwart and former state senator McLeod who was playing seemed the only reason fiddling was even symbolically valuable.

McLeod's fiddling is more appreciated these days at another annual politi- cal affair, the reunion of former state senators in Jackson. In one room, most of the socializing and politicking goes on, and we all eventually eat a traditional cat- fish dinner. In a neighboring smaller room, the caterers lay out enormous chilled prawns and oysters on the half shell (our tax dollars at work), and the musicians set up shop. A few of the attending present and former senators and members of their families pay some degree of attention to the music now and again, and most can- not avoid hearing it at some point, since patronizing the restroom entails passing within a few feet of us. But the end result is not a concert for these politicians but rather a contribution to a down-home atmosphere. What's in it for the musicians? We're paid nothing (apart from access to the pricey snacks), and it's not all that easy to hear one another through the roil of hearty conversation. For us, the value of the occasion is in the energy of the situation and our own take on the symbolism of the occasion: our music is a welcome social lubricant among a crowd of people who are really accomplishing something. The something that they are doing while at the party seems like everyday schmoozing, but this chatter includes power bro- kers influencing one another on matters of great consequence to our state. The essence of the meeting is a heady combination of nostalgia with very real power. This particular music satisfies because the crowd, although not uniformly elderly, does center on men in their seventies who remember when fiddle music was the daily fare for political occasions.

We'll return now to McLeod's time as a member of the senate, the early 1970s. Since doing this job caused him to spend considerable time in the state capital, Jackson, his playing territory expanded to fit that city: "I played in a number of occasions up there. I carried the fiddle with me, and every now and then, there'd be something that came up. I've played for the historical society, some old ladies hav- ing some sort of a meeting. Or play for school younguns, there were just a number of things. I played with the Jackson Symphony, at their Brown Bag Concert." Such occasions for performance point out that fiddling was becoming a music for which much of its audience was polarized by age, the old and the very young, but with both sections of this audience hearing fiddling because it was increasingly consid- ered part of American history. Sometimes a fiddler will be asked to do a school program, a sort of indirect but vivid argument that history isn't just dry facts but can be fun (parallel to ingratiating science class tricks such as freezing a rose with liquid nitrogen, then dramatically shattering the rose on a table). Such programs imply that our ancestors didn't just clear ever more land and gradually refine our democracy; they danced and laughed and courted in a way that may not have always been prim and proper but was rated at worst PG-13. In short, these occasional hours in the classroom paint fiddling as part of purportedly wholesome but lively American history.

For the older, larger section of the newly dichotomous audience, fiddling might well have been part of their aggregate of personal histories, of America as they had experienced it, or at least wished they had. Local historical societies increasingly try to reach beyond their previous major functions of nailing down the facts of local history and helping old folks trace genealogies. One way to add to those services is to present history as full of life, for example, by welcoming a fiddler now and again to revitalize (and perhaps revise) memories of youthful joys, rosy recollections of a time when life was simpler and less morally ambiguous. It is part of the human condition to believe in the good old days and an important part of the current identity of fiddling to share in the embodiment of that nostalgia. In short, the older members of Senator McLeod's audience remember (and "remember") times gone by with the aid of fiddling, while the young are told about these times partly through the medium of fiddling.

McLeod's running for office and serving in the senate during the 1970s led to a modest but real amount of national exposure for him through a pair of performances on the Grand Ole Opry and also to his being part of Mississippi's delegation to the Festival of American Folklife. He played at the Opry at the invitation of Bill Monroe, the father of bluegrass music. His friendship with Monroe resulted from the fortuitous conjunction of the arrival of bluegrass festivals in Mississippi with the process of running for office. When McLeod was arranging for radio spots during his campaign, he had the opportunity to choose what music would run behind his short broadcast speech and found that his favorite tune available at one station was by Monroe. "And that fall [of 1971] we had the first bluegrass festival I'd ever gone to." After McLeod got better acquainted with Monroe at the series of festivals over a half-dozen years, Monroe invited him to perform as his guest at the Grand Ole Opry in 1979.

An earlier trip that resulted from McLeod's visibility as a fiddler and state senator was to the Festival of American Folklife:

> In '74, we went up to Washington. Mississippi was the featured state at the Festival of American Folklife. It was the eighth one they had, and each year they'd feature a state. . . . They took up about 150 Mississippians of various arts and crafts [including

a] chair maker from up here in Greene County . . . I got to go as a fiddler, mainly because I was in the Senate at the time, and they was trying to cater to the legislature to get funding—you know how that kind of works. I don't know if it helped them for me to be in there: I didn't control the legislature or anything like that. But they had good intentions. And I enjoyed going, so I'm not complaining about that.

But they carried a fellow up there from Chunky [near Meridian, Mississippi] . . . as a square dance caller. And I didn't even know that they was carrying a fellow up there as a square dance caller. . . . Coming back [from a concession stand, I saw that] fellow on stage, and he was trying to get people lined up to square dance. They had just skadoodles of people. I don't know if anybody had a count. It was different things going on all over the mall, and a crowd of folks had been there and listened to our music. And [the caller] was trying [to arrange a dance for a group including] a bunch of college kids. . . . I came around the stage: He could see as I came around that I knew something about it. He immediately called on me to lead [the dancers] . . . So we got out there. He was calling the figures. Of course the kids [had] seen dancing to fiddle music, [but] they didn't know anything but skipping. They'd skip from here plumb over to that couch over yonder per skip, and just absolutely mess a dance up, because of the long skip. Everybody can't skip that far you know. It's a skip instead of a dance step. But they saw it done in a movie; I remember seeing the same movie. And it was some Tin-Pan-Alley [director's] idea of a way to put emphasis on it, to show just how hillbilly it was. . . .

And Ralph Rinzler's wife [Kate] was in charge of the stage up there . . . he was putting on a clinic square dancing, up at the end of the mall. And she . . . had seen me calling square dance when we was playing for ourselves, and she asked me would I go up there and call a square dance. There wasn't anybody up there at that stage. So Mickey [Davis, a violist who also fiddles] got a guitar picker, and we walked up there [and led a very successful dance].

Thus, at this national event, McLeod found that the little that well-intended younger urban visitors knew about square dancing had not come from personal experience. Instead, what they knew about the main kind of dance associated with older-style fiddling had been filtered through the media, and thus stylized to exaggerate rustic associations. Of course, many Americans in the baby-boom generation—likely including much of the festival audience—learned some square dancing in physical education classes. I remember this well: a gym with its characteristic palette of odors, mixed attitudes on the parts of the participants, and a scratchy variable-speed turntable from which emanated bad renditions of music seldom connected with the older history of the dance, with fiddling.

McLeod still likes to teach square dancing and insists that it be done with as much historical accuracy as possible. True, this process entails his relinquishing his treasured role of fiddler to someone else, and it is not always easy to find an apt fiddler for this purpose. He does not explain steps over the microphone but teaches as he learned, from within the square. He is the man in the head couple and talks and maneuvers others during the dance.

I witnessed him teaching square dancing recently at the Two Rivers Bluegrass Festival (held in his hometown of Leakesville), as one of the activities away from the stage on an evening early in the festivities. Among the participants were a handful of experienced dancers, avid hobbyists who had learned fancy square dancing as part of a club. This presented its own problem: these dancers wished to "help" McLeod by taking over, by teaching the modern fancy western-style square dance. With the bizarre mix of the absolute beginners and the overly elaborate club dancers, who insisted on enacting their own baroque take on McLeod's instructions, there wasn't much chance for a fruitful or even cheerful learning occasion.

Having an hour of square dance instruction early in this bluegrass festival was part of a trend at these festivals. Yes, bluegrass is a relatively young style of music in a literal sense, but it coalesced in the 1940s and 1950s symbolizing tradition, that is, in reaction to electrified country music. Bluegrass as a family of musical styles has grown to be popular enough that it encompasses considerable variety in mixes of tradition and jazzy virtuosity, but the genre as a whole has never lost its association with rural life and rural ways of thinking. This association persists in symbiosis with the demography of the bluegrass audience. A typical festival lasts several days, with a climax featuring the best touring bands of the event on Friday and Saturday. Young and old attend on the weekend, while the elderly constitute nearly the whole audience during the work week. Many of them are retired couples who tour the country in recreational vehicles, often creating an annual ritual by going from one bluegrass festival to another. They constitute a portable community very interested in the old ways.

The Two Rivers Bluegrass Festival takes place early each April in the Greene County Rural Events Center, the same semi-enclosed dirt-floor building where livestock shows and such are held. Here, as in many rural bluegrass festivals, tradition and bluegrass are to be conjoined very clearly. For instance, the festival food is country cooking in various local guises. One can buy a plate lunch or dinner featuring gumbo, jambalaya, or piles of fried catfish, and the "fried" theme dominates in food stands too. My favorite cart sells chicken-on-a-stick (a shish kebab of chicken, potatoes, and dill pickles, the whole freight train deep-fried). I have not as of this writing mustered the courage to try their deep-fried Oreo cookie dusted with powdered sugar, fearing that this might be a case of gilding the lily. There are numerous craft stands, including a quilt display and demonstration by the Greene County Quilters, several woodworkers, and so on, as well as community service stands, including a book sale supporting the library and a facility to test blood pressure.

McLeod gathers his musician friends and plays at this and several other local festivals on Tuesday, early in a typical festival week. While the event is slowly gathering a head of steam early in the week, various local groups play, usually without pay. The musicians include gospel groups, local bluegrass ensembles, and a teenager attempting broad country comedy in the manner of Jerry Clower. In these acts, down-home credentials and local friendship substitute for the polish of the upcoming weekend's professionals.

That McLeod and friends playing what in essence remains old-time music are relegated to the front edge of the festival, to the edge when oldsters reign in the sparse audience (the square dance instruction is the same early night) is more evidence that his activities as a fiddler appeal to demographic niches clearly defined by age (the old and the young) and by ideology (wholesome, traditional, American). Square dancing as a mainstream community activity had faded in this part of Mississippi during the 1940s and 1950s. Now it's an interesting historical curiosity, hard to sell to busy people with lots of dance choices, and, since McLeod continues to focus on traditional square dance rather than the modern square dance club scene, his receptive audience is small indeed. For a time, he was regularly asked to play for PTA meetings, but invitations ebbed in the mid-1950s. Now, he and other fiddlers are sometimes asked to play school programs, as a sort of living history exhibit, in yet another shift from general entertainment to niche-oriented symbolism.

Early in February of 2002, the ensemble playing at a church affair for old folks included McLeod, his usual guitar accompanist Lee Fulcher, a mandolinist, and me as second guitarist. Groups of seniors were ferried in from rest homes to a large private home in shifts. Members of the church had donated enormous platters of food. We musicians had to overeat twice simply to be polite. The senior citizens feasted too; then some of them gathered around the musicians, who were holding forth in a corner. Of course, the old folks' home as a pervasive institution is itself a rather new thing, a physical embodiment of an age-defined subculture, the generation most interested in fiddling today. When these people who grew up with fiddling as a routine part of life pass from the scene, will the next generation of oldsters be similarly interested? If so, their interest would have to be based on symbolism more than aggregate personal history.

What of other settings that called for fiddlers or at least offered the sounds of fiddling to the public in Greene County, Mississippi, earlier in the century?

Fiddling on local radio ceased when rock music arrived, then returned in a small way with bluegrass, though that faded too after a while. Now, with the advent of cable and satellite TV, the media cater to small niche audiences in addition to the cultural/mercantile mainstream. Bluegrass is a substantial enough subculture to carve out an outpost on the edges of the new media, though fiddling outside of bluegrass misses the cut in even the richest satellite programming. And, of course, anyone can purchase a few recordings of fiddling by visiting giant record stores in large cities. But even the largest such store will just have a CD or two of fiddling that isn't allied to bluegrass. Those who wish to buy contest or old-time fiddle recordings can locate some in specialty stores through the internet (County Records has the best selection), or, ideally, physically travel to the fiddle subculture, that is, visit fiddle contests and bluegrass festivals with their sales of proprietary recordings (the CDs of their own playing that performers truck to such occasions).

How about fiddle contests? McLeod played at them regularly for fifty years, but their flavor continually evolved, so his tune choices for contests have changed in response. In his first contest, held in Fruitdale, Alabama, in 1949, he played "Pop Goes the Weasel" holding his fiddle not just under his chin, but also upside down, behind his back, and so forth. That contest still retained much of the feel of the 1920s contests described earlier in this chapter, but times were changing. Later, McLeod did well in a contest through a politically astute tune choice: "In the playoff, I played a waltz, and I played 'Carroll County Blues.' And I was in territory close to where 'Carroll County Blues' supposedly emerged."

When McLeod, following his teacher's advice, began using "Ragtime Annie" in contests, he was choosing a tune that plenty of players all over the United States know and play. But he discovered that other traditional Mississippi fiddlers found his version suspect, in part because a flourish with which he opened the high strain was deemed unusual but even more so because of the inclusion of Jode Denmark's third strain (one that McLeod hadn't often heard elsewhere, because it is found almost exclusively in Texas versions). Yes, that strain does appear in the 1922 commercial recording by Texan Eck Robertson, and that may well be why it was in the version McLeod learned, that of Jode Denmark. Robertson's recordings were among the fiddle recordings that were sold all over the United States during the 1920s and 1930s but that subsequently became much harder to find. This efflorescence was during Denmark's youth. Denmark's repertoire was eclectic, just as Eck Robertson's had been, and just as McLeod's would be.

Today, with a lower geographical density of fiddlers and with fiddlers meeting and hearing each other in contests or festivals more often than in each other's homes, more of a purist attitude has emerged, one not very tolerant of heterogeneity of repertoire or style, despite admiring the eclectic repertoires of fiddlers of the past. Contests, in order to be coherent, need to be divided into categories, and these are often defined by style. Thus, many contests in the Southeast place fiddlers in either the old-time category or that of bluegrass (both are really families of styles). Elsewhere in the country, a contest may have old-time style separated out from the array of newer solo fiddle styles that are centered on Texas contest style. Such segregations by style have beneficial effects. By protecting styles possessing less "ear candy" than the contest-oriented styles, these separate categories of competition preserve variety of style. And since these styles are of different vintages and appeal to performers of different ages in some parts of the country, the separation allows for the exposure of a broader sweep of the history of American fiddling during contests. McLeod could have easily won more at contests by having become more of a modern old-time purist, that is, if he had sought out an old-time style self-consciously and meticulously avoided any influences of bluegrass or of Texas fiddling. But that would have been true neither to the letter nor to the spirit of the fiddle tradition he inherited in Leakesville, Mississippi. And his own cumulative approach to shaping a repertoire and style strikes me as an unusually careful—neither labored nor precious but genuinely nuanced—mix of respect for what he learned from his principal teacher, Jode Denmark, with how fiddling evolved in his own life after his apprenticeship years. He reflects on his music more than many fiddlers do but does not obsess about any aspect of symbol or sound. It's fun, it's history, it's part of him, and it's a way to share this whole package with family, friends, and also with strangers, who thus are more likely to become friends.

Would McLeod pass on tunes in the same sort of intimate environments in which he learned them? The simple answer is no, but the reasons are complex. The chance of keeping fiddling vital in the family and in the neighborhood would depend on some continuity in several spheres, in how daily life in rural areas does or does not encourage extended families to stay reasonably intact and to interact regularly, to what degree fiddling can be heard on a regular basis outside of the home, and whether a musical child would see fiddling as a fun choice for a hobby.

Of George Cecil's children, a daughter lives at home and a son lives very nearby in McLeod's former home. Another child lives in Mobile, Alabama, about a hour away, several are in Atlanta, one teaches at Delta State (about two hours away), and a daughter has retired with her air force husband in Hawaii. Since Leakesville has neither the natural resources nor felicitous location that would encourage further growth, having more children in this large family depart than stay isn't surprising and in fact simply reflects national demographic trends. But, unsurprising or not, this doesn't help in fostering any sorts of oral tradition within such families. In fact, none of McLeod's kids took up the fiddle. There were so many other kinds of music around to enjoy as they grew up (a much wider selection than in their parents' childhoods), and fiddling symbolized patterns of life from which they grew away. Will an apprentice surface outside of the family but within the community, someone who will visit George Cecil the way he visited Jode Denmark? This hasn't happened yet; aspiring musicians are more likely to take up rock guitar, or, if particularly interested in tradition, a bluegrass instrument, which may or may not be the fiddle. Again, this is just a matter of demography-based odds working out: for the tradition-oriented student of music, there are a half-dozen other instruments in bluegrass bands to choose from, and, in fact, a fair number of bands don't even have a fiddle.

In a sample fortnight, from September 28 through October 12 of 2002, George Cecil McLeod fiddled in quite a variety of venues. His main guitar accompanist for nearly thirty years has been Lee Fulcher, a retired postal worker who lives in Wiggins, about an hour's drive from Leakesville (they met at a bluegrass festival in the mid-1970s); however, McLeod often invites others to join in. At the annual McLeod family reunion in Leakesville, he, Lee, and I played in a corner of a church fellowship hall while well over one hundred family members visited with each other and filled their plates with home cooking. Some folks listened and some didn't, but even those who hadn't seemed to have been paying attention later expressed sincere gratitude; it was clear that symbol as well as sound had mattered. The Pine Belt's dulcimer club invited him to fiddle a few numbers at their weekly meeting in Hattiesburg and also to join in with their group numbers when possible. ("We play in the key of D," we were told at this low-pressure jam.) On the way to that event, he and Fulcher stopped off at the county hospital and played for the ward on which Mrs. McLeod was recuperating from hip surgery. He and Fulcher performed one evening at a local restaurant, and they also competed at the state fiddle contest held during the state fair. Last, we three would have played during the opening evening of a local bluegrass festival, but back-to-back tropical storms caused the festival to be canceled. This was an especially busy time for McLeod as fiddler, but the venues were representative.

McLeod continues to do his best to continue to represent his local fiddle tradition and considers it both an honor and a pleasure to do so. To what degree is his case representative? It does seem that most of the venues in which he now plays welcome him partly because he is a fiddler but more because they enjoy his charisma and wish to honor him as an individual. His personal history illustrates broad shifts of fiddling in American culture, first moving from normal entertainment in a very rural area to being viewed as a fun illustration of history, then to being the stable linchpin of a fiddle-based subculture, the fiddle contest environment.

CHAPTER TWO

Modern Fiddle Contests
The Competition Itself

These days, most active American fiddlers attend several fiddle contests every year. Since dances accompanied by live fiddling have become uncommon in most parts of the United States, and no major alternative opportunities for public performance have emerged, contests are the main public venue for fiddling. These events build social and musical alliances, inspire practice, and help shape repertoires and styles. But every fiddler has mixed feelings about each contest that he frequents and, indeed, about whether competition is good for him or healthy for fiddling in general. In fact, many fiddlers and other musicians who attend contests regularly never compete. Some of the most avid performers concentrate exclusively on what most musicians do when not on stage: jamming and socializing. Nevertheless, the competition itself, pernicious or not, is indispensable: without it, fiddlers and their fans would seldom gather and interact in numbers comparable to those we see at contests.

This chapter concerns contests as competition. It's about what contests claim to be about. The next chapter concerns the jamming, eating, camping, purchasing, talking, and laughing—that is, the rest (and arguably the essence) of what fiddle contests are about. Some readers will read the two chapters straight through, but others will be more comfortable going back and forth between them.

The most overt business of fiddle contests includes where they take place, how the competitors are parceled out into competition brackets, and how the events proceed from start to finish. Certain aspects of contest format and flavor are basic; the general description of the contest in Tuscaloosa opening chapter 1 will resonate with all of them. But there's significant variation too. I will narrate two different yet representative small contests, then look at three large and important ones.

Small Contests at Fairs

Folk music competition in the United States was at first a series of local affairs. Today, despite better roads and vehicles, increased leisure, and more disposable income, all contests retain regional emphases and flavors, even the handful that claim a national scope. I'll first examine a very local affair, a contest that has always been part of a state fair. Such contests echo history since, back when fiddling was a regular ingredient of mainstream entertainment, it routinely entered public view in connection with general local festivities. Now that fiddling has become a small-ish subculture, the small "dependent" contests retain a special role in recruiting new fans and new fiddlers. Plenty of Americans who know little about fiddling brush against the fiddle world just because they stroll through a county or state fair at just the right time.

I moved with my family to Mississippi in the summer of 2000 and attended the Mississippi state fiddle contest in Jackson for the first time that fall. I did immediately feel at home at this contest. It fits enough norms that anyone accustomed to such events will know what is going on immediately. The official title is quite grand: Mississippi State Fiddlers and Liars Contest. But the word "state" in that title is an exaggeration. Indeed, lots of contests claim to draw on larger geographical areas than they actually do. It is true that some fiddle contests with the word "state" in their names attract well within their own state and also from neighboring ones, such as the healthy Kentucky state contest and remarkably influential Texas state contest. But the Mississippi "state" contest remains small. In terms of vernacular culture, Mississippi divides into the delta plus three horizontal bands corresponding to geographic areas, that is, good-sized hills in the north, smaller hills and the piney woods in the center, and the gulf coast. The gulf coast has few fiddlers, and fiddlers from the north generally prefer contests in the nearby flourishing fiddle environments of Tennessee and Alabama, where prize money is good. In the end, well over 90 percent of the participants in this "state" fiddle contest actually live in the center of the state, in or near Jackson, or immediately south in the piney woods region.

The contest costs little to arrange; the fair commission's main investment is a modest total purse of about four thousand dollars. And this contest suits the overall mood of the state fair, which is an old-fashioned weeklong composite of events, an annual outpost of older rural life and entertainment. The whole family can enjoy not just the scruffy carnival but the all-important livestock shows, smaller but ideologically congruent displays such as an antique and classic car show and molasses making, and big musical shows centered on performers whose main draw is the nostalgia they evoke (in 2001 including Paul Revere and the Raiders, Ronnie

Millsap, and Gary Lewis and the Playboys). And the main way to organize large numbers of similar items at the fair is the contest, whether the competitors are livestock, local "talent," racing pigs, "pulling" horses and mules, dance drill teams, cheerleaders, 4-H Sweethearts, painters of landscapes and such, or fiddlers and liars. In short, this fiddle contest fits comfortably in both the administrative pattern of relaxed, cheerful, small-scale competition and the relentlessly wholesome flavor of the parade of musical events.

This contest takes place on the last Saturday of the fair. The performers are parceled out into divisions following regional norms, some brackets borrowed from the southeastern pattern (where competition brackets are defined by performance medium) and some from the west (where the assembly of fiddlers is subdivided by age). The "liars," an unusual category (a "lie" being a tall tale), appear individually between divisions. In the 2003 contest, there were performing, in this order, eight fiddlers aged up to eight, thirteen aged nine to twelve, nine aged thirteen to twenty-five, five aged twenty-six to fifty-six, and four aged fifty-seven and over. After lunch, the winners in those categories faced each other in a "fiddle off." Then we heard from handfuls of players of, in turn, bluegrass banjo, harmonica, and miscellaneous instruments, then a few string bands.

The organizers gather the contestants into brackets that are roughly the same size, hence the mathematically eccentric groupings of fiddlers by age. The most narrowly defined bracket, for children aged nine to twelve, is nevertheless also the largest every year. Indeed, this contest is primarily for kids: roughly three-fourths of the fiddlers are under eighteen every year, and few are skilled. That most are new to the craft is made clear by who accompanies them. Some have their parents on stage, but most have their teachers supporting them on guitar. Two studios dominate. Tim Avalon, a solid professional fiddler proficient in various American styles and in modern Irish fiddling, teaches most of the kids who actually sound like fiddlers. Even more youngsters study with a couple who are classical musicians but know little about fiddling. It's common nationwide for violin students in the Suzuki method to be dragged to fiddle contests: any chance to perform is "good for them." But, however cute these kids may be, and however valuable to them the experience may be, when they arrive in droves the beginners' portion of any fiddle contest becomes excruciating for the audience. If these children skipped this contest, would it shrink out of existence? Or would more real fiddlers show up? Will some of the budding violinists be seduced by fiddling? That is, is the Suzuki onslaught an effective recruiting tool for the fiddle world? Is sitting through a stultifying parade of maiden efforts worth it?

Partly owing to this ubiquitous friction between the classical violin and fiddle worlds, and partly owing to limited jamming and socializing opportunities, contests of this type tend to stay small and to be just plain poor contests. They remain important, however, in advertising fiddling to new audiences. No fiddle contest is very well publicized outside the area where it takes place, and often there's little publicity of any kind beyond word-of-mouth and fliers at the registration booth of other contests. The Mississippi State Contest is announced each year in Jackson's largest newspaper in just one tiny article. Thus, in general, if you're not already in the fiddle contest world, you're unlikely to hear about it. But people who come to such fairs to sample the carnival rides or the livestock shows may well stroll by the contest tent, hear fiddling, and perhaps be drawn in.

There's no printed program at this contest, and judges don't perform; they likely can't, at least not on all of the instruments they are called upon to judge. They are generally middle-aged to older men, three of them, judging absolutely all of the performance categories. At such low-budget events, all three probably live nearby and thus don't need hotel rooms or mileage allowances, just a minimal honorarium. Although most judges have some musical experience, they may not be fiddlers. For instance, the announcer introduced the chief judge in 2000 as "Music Director at Holly Grove Baptist Church. He has a bachelor's degree from the University of Southern Mississippi with a double major in sports administration and social studies. He's a social studies instructor at Magee High School and presently coaches Magee High School's boys' basketball team and girls' softball team. His music interests include playing the piano." Although such judges are by contemporary performance-based standards underqualified, there's something attractively old-fashioned about their selection. They are the sorts of solid citizens who judged fiddling early in the twentieth century, when one could expect that most everyone would have heard plenty of fiddling and that qualified judges could be plucked out of the general populace on the bases of probity and community status. But the results of choosing judges by these formerly effective means can be mixed today, since plenty of musical prominent citizens know little or nothing about fiddling. Sadly, at this and similar contests, broad technical fluency has come to trump tradition: classically trained young violinists who have memorized a few fiddle tunes often triumph over rougher-sounding but more authentic fiddlers.

As the 2002 Mississippi contest wound down, George Cecil McLeod and I sat together, and I listened to his justified grousing at the judges' decisions. A fine woman violinist had prepared only one fiddle tune and was caught without anything to play at the fiddle-off between the winners of the age-based categories of competition. She triumphed by improvising a Paganini-esque fantasy on "Old Joe Clark" that had absolutely nothing to do with fiddling beyond the barely recognizable kernel of a tune she had employed as a point of departure. The judges, and much of the audience, appreciated her wonderful technique and musicianship and were willing to overlook her lack of acquaintance with fiddling. George Cecil was far from the only real fiddler unhappy with the results, but he and the others kept this glitch in perspective: what really mattered was that they had gotten together and jammed, gossiped, felt good about the values they expressed by fiddling.

Independent Small Contests Funding Local Philanthropy

The annual Ashe County Old Time Fiddler's and Bluegrass Convention takes place the first Saturday each August in Ashe County Recreational Park in the town of West Jefferson, in the mountainous northwest corner of North Carolina. The drive of several hours from my former home in North Carolina's Piedmont gradually assumes more curves and elevation, passing through tobacco fields, then Christmas tree farms, and finally traversing the eastern Continental Divide before entering West Jefferson. A banner announcing the contest greets all entering the city: even such small contests are big tourist events in little towns.

The Ashe Rotary Club sponsors the contest. Such organizations grew out of earlier informal neighborhood cooperation, that is, the casual alliances that eased barn raisings and harvests. The county's need for a hospital inspired the organization of the Ashe County chapter of the Rotary Club in 1938. The club then helped with a bean market, a community tobacco warehouse, and, in the late 1960s, the building of a local airport. They were responsible for the creation of Ashe Park, which opened about 1970. Now their major thrust is in financing modest but locally significant college scholarships. In 1967, the club began an annual horse show to support this (and to stimulate the horse raising industry). When sufficient dirt had been trucked in to level and dry swampy areas at Ashe Park, the show moved there. After a few years, and mixed success, the horse show was abandoned in favor of the fiddle convention.

The Rotarians remain responsible for all work at the event; the fact that these workers volunteer their time accounts for much of the money raised. They first solicit ads to go in a printed program more than sixty pages long. There's enough relevant content to convince attendees to page through the booklet: three pages of photographs of music making, the convention rules (a half page), a page or so each on the history of the local Rotary Club here and on the growth of the convention, a page listing club members, and a very important page of photographs of the eight to twelve scholarship winners from the three local high schools. The rest of the booklet consists of ads, many of which are for Rotary members' companies, of course, and match the local yellow pages well, showing that the whole community supports this convention. As August approaches, Rotarians groom the grounds and reassemble the small stage. During the contest they take tickets and sell sandwiches and contest T-shirts. Early on Sunday morning after the convention, there they are again, picking up garbage with such exuberance that we tired campers feign good moods too, and get dressed and move on.

The setting for the contest is beautiful, a flattish area within forested rolling hills. A few dozen ranks of benches face the small, covered stage, though most of the thousand plus audience members bring folding chairs or blankets to sit on, as is the custom at outdoor festivals. One or two small platforms on the grass between the stage and the audience offer flatfoot dancers a place to practice during the competition. In earlier eras, fiddling had a mixed reputation, since the dancing with which it was then primarily associated might well lead to energetic courting, drinking, and even brawling. Now families attend fiddle contests like this one, bringing coolers and dogs, which they leash to their chairs, and the dancing is as innocent as it is vigorous.

Here, as throughout the upper Southeast, fiddle contests are divided into categories by what instruments contestants play. Also, this part of the country is band-oriented: the climax contest brackets are for old-time bands and for bluegrass bands. Having separate categories for band types keeps the old-time bands and local styles from being overshadowed by the fancier bluegrassers, and, not incidentally, insures broad participation and a substantial gate. In the bands called "old-time," a fiddle and clawhammer banjo duo will be supplemented with a guitar or two, a bass, and perhaps some other acoustic stringed instrument, while in the somewhat larger bluegrass bands, a mandolin will supplement or supplant the fiddle, and banjoists fingerpick Scruggs-style. There are also both old-time and bluegrass categories for solo fiddle and for solo banjo. While most instrumentalists compete both within their band and as performers on their particular instruments, if they're in a band, they are *judged* as soloists at the same time that their band is performing and being judged as an ensemble.

Individual competitors and bands line up backstage in no particular order, although bands tend to line up later than soloists, and most singers perform early (bands play two tunes, individuals just one). In order to illustrate the general feel of the progress of the evening, I list the competitors at the 1996 Ashe County Old Time Fiddler's and Bluegrass Convention after this paragraph, abbreviating, for the solo instruments, old-time as ot and bluegrass as b, to save space.

song, song, ot fiddle, song, song, song, song, song, mandolin, song, song, b banjo, song, song, song, song, song, song, song, song, song, song, song, ot banjo, b band,

b fiddle, song, b fiddle, mandolin, ot fiddle, b band, b band, song, song, ot fiddle,
guitar, ot band, ot fiddle, ot banjo, ot banjo, b band, junior flatfoot dancing . . . ,
b band, ot band, b band, b band, ot banjo, ot banjo, ot band, ot band, ot fiddle,
ot band, b band, ot band, ot band, guitar, ot band, ot band, b fiddle, b band, ot band,
b band, b band, ot band, b fiddle, b band, b banjo, b band, b fiddle, ot band, b band,
guitar, b band, b band, ot band, senior flatfoot dancing . . .

Emcees warn inexperienced attendees that the contest may "start slow" but
promise that excitement will build later, when the bands play. Indeed, the music is
more and more stirring as the hours pass, but much of the cumulative power of the
evening has to do with how accustomed the audience is to seeing precisely these
bands. In some cases, performers are audience members' neighbors. For instance,
Rita Scott plays fiddle with the Appalachian Mountain Girls, a group of musical
friends that competes at all of the nearby conventions, and has sometimes been
the "house band" here, playing warm-up sets early in the day and accompanying
the flatfoot dancers. She lives right there in Jefferson and works at a small publisher downtown. Her kids are in school with the children of folks in the audience. Other groups have become part of the community simply through annual
performances here and at nearby contests; they are like relatives that one sees a few
times a year. The Roan Mountain Hilltoppers, from Tennessee, may not be day-
to-day acquaintances of anyone at the convention, but they compete here most
years and are well liked. In 1990, old Joe Birchfield fiddled, and all members of the
band shared his last name. In 1996, when Joe was gone, his nephew Bill had shifted
from guitar to fiddle, and the new guitarist was not a Birchfield; my neighbors in
the audience lamented Joe's passing. Balancing that loss was a gain in the family
cohesiveness of the Slate Mountain Ramblers: teenaged Marsha Bowman had become skilled enough to replace a non-family member on banjo—again, occasion-
ing audience comments—while her father, Richard, still fiddled and her mother,
Barbara, still played bass.

Each of the cases just mentioned concerned old-time bands, which tend to
be based locally in especially small towns, most with populations under 1,200,
towns where everybody really does know everybody else and their doings. In general, the bluegrass bands were based in bigger cities than were the old-time bands.
The names of all of the bands have a rural flavor, but the names of the old-time
bands more frequently have a local focus: Pilot Mountain Bobcats, Walnut Hill
Old-Time Band, and so on. Fiddle-based bands in the smallest towns may choose
old-time music over bluegrass for practical, demographic reasons. These bands
just need two genuinely skilled players to do a creditable job—the fiddler and the

clawhammer banjoist—while bluegrass bands require most of their five or more musicians to be able to take creditable solo breaks. But it is more compelling that, in the words of Barbara Allen, "Southerners' attachment to home—their sense of place—is perhaps the hallmark of their regional identity"; this is "most apparent in the rural neighborhoods that have historically been the seedbeds of southern folk culture." It therefore comes as no surprise that the most traditional bands are here exhibiting the strongest attachment to place. The bluegrass bands' regional to national orientation is reflected in more general names of bands: Mountain Drive (no particular mountain), 20th-century Bluegrass, Southern Breeze, and so on.

The evenings, the nights, and the early mornings gradually wind down. Our elder daughter, Kate, spends most of her time on the dancing boards. The first year we took Ellen, she wasn't walking yet but really wanted to be with her sister. She would crawl toward the dancers determinedly. After a few minutes, she was nearly in range of the flying feet, and I would fetch her back to our seats. And off she would go again. The repeated slow and steady progress away alternated with quicker trips back much like the patterned motion of a typewriter carriage, and our neighbors on the front row enjoyed clocking the sequence.

Near the end of the evening, larger donated items are raffled off: such strategies keep tired audiences reasonably intact at long contests nationwide. Sandwiches at the concession stand slip to half price; then the stand closes. Emcees warn us that rowdy behavior will result in removal by the police, but who's got the energy to misbehave? Finally, winners are announced, and tired cheers and cynical snorts mix evenly in the audience. Winners generally come from nearby, though a few lower prizes go to excellent bands from farther away. This pattern holds year after year at all small fiddle contests in this general area.

What are we to make of the long-standing pattern of mildly preferential treatment given to local bands at the Ashe County contest and others nearby? The judges are knowledgeable and do intend to be fair. But when ranking is hard, several factors incline judges toward local players and bands. These judges live near these events and need to be able to look local players in the eye all year. They know not just how local bands sounded at the contest but how well they play at their best. Bands that win at given contests are apt to come back the next year. In an age when old-time players have numerous opportunities to hear bands from hundreds of miles away, and when a stress-free two-hour drive to a contest covers a distance that devoured several days not too long ago, a slight local favoritism encourages bands to concentrate on attending local contests and to emulate their nearest neighbors' style. In brief, this reinforces local identity.

Too Much Success: The Largest Fiddlers "Convention"

"You'll really enjoy it if you don't freak out," said the woman in the lawn chair next to mine. We were at one large fiddle convention (in Clifftop, West Virginia, during August 2001) discussing the next week's contest, the biggest one in the eastern United States, in Galax, Virginia. She had been to the Old Fiddlers Convention many times, but I hadn't attended yet. Every year, I took my family to the convention in Ashe County, North Carolina, discussed above. This took place the week before Galax. Then we would go the weekend *after* Galax to the small convention in Fries, Virginia. The reputation of the Galax convention was more forbidding than enticing: all of the drawbacks of festival gigantism were said to be virulently active. As I finally drove toward it, I tried to forget my Clifftop companion's parting shot: "Before we left Galax last year, we were swimming in shit!" Rainstorms had immobilized hundreds of RVs, many of whose owners chose to void sanitation systems into the muck. The contest organizers had to muster a fleet of tractors to free up attendees' vehicles for the noisy (and noisome) journey home. What an image my Clifftop friend had conjured! But despite these memories, she intended to attend Galax herself once again, so I went ahead too.

The city of Galax occupies a lovely valley in the Blue Ridge Mountains of southwest Virginia. The word "Galax" honors a local type of waxy green leaf called the galax leaf, which is valued in floral arrangements and durable enough to be shipped nationwide (local agriculture now centers on the Christmas tree business, just as in Jefferson, North Carolina). Although the population of Galax has hovered at about seven thousand for decades, the flavor of the area has gradually changed. Tourism now dominates the city's economy and public image. Galax's outskirts match the edges of most American small towns: one negotiates a husk of service stations, a Wal-Mart, and fast food restaurants to reach inner circles of residences (plus unlovely patches of industry) before finding the historic downtown. A few glances reveal a population neither affluent nor impoverished, one mostly white but with a sizeable black presence and a growing Latin minority.

Felts Park, the contest's downtown site, encompasses twenty-eight acres, a three-thousand-seat grandstand, and three baseball fields. A stage at the side of a tent (constructed anew each year) looks across a stretch of sand to the grandstand. The interior of the tent houses registration for competition and shelters the first dozen meters of long lines of musicians waiting to play. The sandy area between stage and grandstand swiftly fills with some 500 folding chairs belonging to audience members. Groups rope their chairs together to discourage claim-jumpers. Pedestrian corridors remain between the ranks of folding chairs and a dozen food stands (plus sales booths for instruments, CDs, and so on). The rest of the

Figure 2. At the campground in Felts Park in Galax, Virginia, in 2001, old-time fiddler Richard Bowman is next to the family camper, jamming with a rotating group of instrumentalists. The fiddlers tend to stay put, and the other players move from camp to camp.

Figure 3. Another fine old-time fiddler at Galax, Rita Scott is in front of her tent-on-wheels, 2001.

park fills with RVs, campers and a handful of tents, literally hundreds of portable dwellings.

Campers line up in the wee hours of Sunday morning to get into the park so that they can set up their temporary quarters near the end of the park where the stage sits, and also so that given families can camp near their friends. A golf cart piloted by a Shriner—active members of the Moose who administer the event are not numerous enough to fully staff it—leads one RV or pickup-cum-camper after another to the next available chalked rectangle, and Felts Park slowly fills. Campers level their vehicles, provide shade by tying out an endless mosaic of tarps, set out tables and chairs, and are ready for a week of talking, jamming, talking, competing, and talking. On the Monday through Friday of the event, the contest begins at 7:00 P.M.; despite the high elevation, it's just too hot to be very energetic outdoors earlier.

The Galax Moose Lodge #733 first arranged the contest in 1935 (then with the help of the local PTA, later with the Chamber of Commerce, and now with the help of other convivial volunteer organizations). A vernacular music contest was selected for their fund-raiser because there was plenty of old-time music still being made in the area. As the event mushroomed, it attracted contestants from further and further away. By 1958, a competitor in the "novelty" category came all the way from New York City. By the 1960s, lots of college kids and counterculture types were attending from big cities. "The hippies used to bathe naked in the river. We enjoyed that," an older local woman told me.

Just as in West Jefferson and at most contests in the Southeast, fiddling at Galax is ensemble-oriented (old-time bands and bluegrass bands), and most competition brackets—all but the rather new youth bracket scheduled first—reflect the instrument one commands or the ensemble in which one participates. A given instrumentalist may compete once alone and once in a band. The competition brackets are, however, crude devices in certain ways. It's artificial in both old-time music and bluegrass to extract soloists from an ensemble situation, and the binary division of performance into old-time and bluegrass can be simplistic. In particular, the banjo styles that a player grew up with may not belong clearly to one or the other stylistic world. Some old-time banjo styles lack the "claw-hammer" down-picking motion that produces the style-specific percussive sound and way of shaping melodies. Old banjo styles that feature up-picking (the more "normal" finger motions in which the strings are played by fingers flexing toward the palm of the hand) are less easy to distinguish from bluegrass styles, though the rhythmic effect remains distinctive. I've been told by such old-time banjoists that they play clawhammer style only for contests, feeling that they will otherwise be graded down.

The last problem with the use of discrete brackets of competition at southeastern contests concerns scheduling. When a performance style such as old-time fiddling or medium such as dobro is isolated, that pleases a targeted audience, but folks not sharing that specific enthusiasm may leave, resulting in less of a feeling of general community and more one of a patchwork of smaller communities. A truly large audience assembles only for the two band categories on Friday and Saturday nights.

The announcers are meticulously homespun local radio personalities: "Friends and neighbors, Clarence is going to play you a tune I'm sure you'll like. It's 'Sally Ann.' Go ahead, Clarence." As the musicians play (some deadpan serious, others grinning) some audience members listen intently while others chat, smoke like chimneys, and snack incessantly. Brief applause and a few yells follow each musician's brief turn on the stage (under three minutes!). A given competitor will have little idea how they did beyond the impression yielded by the strength of crowd response until the wee hours of Sunday morning, when the winners are announced and prize money awarded.

Whom do we see on stage, and what quality of performance do we hear? As in West Jefferson, the majority of participants are from small towns or the countryside in the Upper South. I discern no pattern in their professions, though northern and city folks constitute a stable minority among the old-time musicians (the politically liberal doctors, lawyers, and so forth, who have sedately assumed the counterculture mantle formerly and more dramatically worn by hippie visitors). Men outnumber women considerably, though the genders even out among the youngest participants. Dress is adamantly informal, though some of the bluegrassers aspire to matching shirts. Some groups are made up of musicians that met through that activity, discovered that they were of congruent abilities and personalities, and then became friends. But at least as many ensembles began as friendship groups or families, then plugged into the hobby already cultivated by one of their number. Family ensembles are common and conspicuous; their youngest members inspire ardent applause, whether they are already accomplished musicians or not. A few of the musicians of any age here are clearly beginners, while several performers are outright superlative. Most are simply competent, roughly as musical and agile as the members of an average community orchestra. To play these dance tunes at an acceptable level is just not that difficult. The essential requirements are physical vigor, good sense of time, and some sense of pitch. If you can dance and can sing, you can also likely master most of the instruments and play this music with a reasonable amount of practice; thus, the repertoire lends itself to an egalitarian ethic. And the repertoire for average and highly skilled practitioners is essentially the same. In the end, all fiddle contests are ironically egalitarian. They produce winners, but you cannot have winners without having losers. Neither old-time nor bluegrass music supports many musicians as professionals. Bluegrass has a broader audience base, and there are a fair number of both full-time professionals and talented amateurs garnering pay many a weekend. But few of those good groups attend Galax. Instead, while some bluegrass bands do stand out as dynamic and tight, most are pedestrian. The average quality of the old-time performances at Galax is higher.

In short, at the Old Fiddlers Convention put on by the Moose Lodge in Galax, Virginia, great music and a relaxed venue to socialize balance uneasily with poor facilities, perfunctory competition, and a strained relationship with the contest organizers, thus presenting positive and negative lessons about how such events can be structured. But to regular attendees, the negative aspects are akin to fraternity hazing. Once you endure the arrival marathon, and get your camp set up, and if don't mind the paucity of showers or take the mechanical nature of the official contest too seriously, then you enter a brotherhood of fellow sufferers who have a tremendous time jamming and visiting for a full week. When I did finally go to this climax event of the old-time fiddler's year, I did love it, though there were indeed moments when I did nearly "freak out."

A "National" Contest?

The annual contest in Weiser, Idaho, looms large in many fiddlers' lives. While most attendees are from the West, contingents travel from Texas, from Alabama, and from farther away, regularly including a fiddler or two from Alaska, from Florida, from New York, even from abroad. The contest is billed as the National Oldtime Fiddlers' Contest. It's debatable what "national" means here, but this is arguably the largest American fiddle contest and certainly the one that is the most broadly publicized and most efficiently run.

Weiser, a small, quiet town located close to the Oregon border northwest of Boise, rests in a comma between mountain ranges. Of more than five thousand inhabitants, most remain blue-collar whites, although a growing minority are of Mexican descent. The town's main employers still depend on agriculture (Champion Home Builders and Appleton Produce food processors), though many citizens commute out of town to work at a casino or in the outdoor recreation business. Idaho fosters a cowboy heritage and outdoor orientation in its festivals. Weiser's own annual cycle of celebrations follows the regional pattern closely; they put on rodeos, an aircraft fly-in, an art show (mostly of landscapes), and the biggest annual event, this fiddle contest.

Just as in many parts of America, there were fiddle contests in Weiser in the 1910s through the 1930s, then a long lapse. A fiddler belonging to the Chamber of Commerce, Blaine Stubblefield, pestered the chamber until funding was found for the initial incarnation of this contest, the Northwest Mountain Fiddlers' Contest, which debuted in 1953. It wasn't easy to get it started. Sharon Poulson Graf relates how Stubblefield first contacted local fiddlers to see if there was a critical mass of them who would be interested in coming (1999, 74). Her history of the contest focuses on the conflicts inherent in the "dual purpose" of the event, to preserve a tradition and to entertain an audience (78). For instance, a time limit for contestants' playing was in place from the beginning, since the organizing committee "was advised that without one some fiddlers were known to play until the cows come home" (83). Dance-oriented fiddlers, who were accustomed to playing until a lengthy dance was concluded, were newly on stage following rules that their customary ways of shaping tunes might not fit. But eventually, Texas-derived contest fiddle styles would dominate here and throughout the West.

The growth of this contest, its differentiation through adding ever more categories of competition defined by age, its eventual claim to being the "national" contest, and its current preeminence in much of the fiddle world, all stem from one factor. It wasn't that fiddling was especially strong in this part of Idaho or that the location could ever claim to have special convenience or innate appeal. It was the constant, energetic, and intelligent engagement of the Chamber of Commerce that made the difference. From the beginning, the chamber has regularly discussed and refined the event in systematic consultation with northwestern fiddlers and with organizers of other contests. They have made visitors' stays in Weiser as easy and convivial as possible and made the process of competition as systematic and fair as they could.

The musicians that come to Weiser are quite a diverse group, with a far higher percentage of city-dwelling enthusiasts than prevails in Texas or points east (with the exception of the festival in Clifftop, West Virginia, which attracts lots of old-timey urban revivalists). The first official event of the 2001 contest underlined this variety. At 4:00 P.M. on Sunday, fiddlers who were already settled in could meet and quiz the judges. This was intended to be informative and reassuring, but the meeting revealed potential problems too. Many questions and answers simply reaffirmed the usual, common-sense feel for what tunes and styles are permissible. Several fiddlers wanted to know which peripheral techniques would be allowed, such as "hokum bowing" (OK if integral to an accepted tune, such as is the case with "Beaumont Rag") and harmonics (same story, with "Whistler's Waltz"). But one judge said, "When in doubt, leave it out." The word "tasteful" emerged repeatedly. Rules aimed at ensuring efficient turnover of fiddlers on stage were reemphasized: If your three tunes totaled over four minutes and ten seconds, penalties would be assessed (which did happen and was noted on publicly available scoring summaries). Also, no tuning was to take place on stage. Yet other questions did not allow for simple answers. One fiddler asked: "Our tempos have gotten progressively faster. Is that what we want?" One judge replied that any tune must be "danceable," but several others thought faster was better if other desirable technical qualities did not suffer. Judge Mark Ralph emphasized drive, Daniel Carwile clarity, and Keith Wilson control. Arizona fiddler and teacher Pete Rolland wanted to know if obscure tunes would have an equal chance to garner good scores. Judge Donna Reuter answered that variety could be refreshing but that the judges must be able to hear that a given tune fit a given bracket in the competition (that is, clearly be a breakdown, waltz, or tune of choice readily comparable with the other tunes in the same category). Pete countered that the "folk process doesn't have clear boundaries" (a rather academic phrasing, startling in this setting). At the end of the question-and-answer session, the judges were asked if any of them had anything they desired to express. Daniel Carwile volunteered that he would welcome some creativity in versions of tunes but within boundaries of good taste: he didn't want to be asking "where's the melody?" All in all, this session acquainted curious fiddlers with judges' opinions—a valuable service—and also with the considerable variety within those views, which must have been sobering.

The contest proper started early the next morning and would fill five days and evenings (roughly 8:00 A.M. to 11:00 P.M., with brief meal breaks), plus a long Saturday evening. I don't believe that anyone except for me was foolish enough to sit through absolutely every fiddler's time at bat, but many contestants (and their families) listened to their compatriots in their age and thus competition bracket, and the gym was always crowded for rounds of the "nationals" bracket (which occurred roughly once a day). Each competitor had to be in the chaotic practice room a bit ahead of time, then, as his or her turn approached, would be efficiently guided into a holding area and then down a corridor to the stage, a raised platform smack-dab in the middle of the audience, rather like at a boxing match. The single microphone used during the contest fiddling was simply raised and lowered on a pulley to suit a given fiddler's height. The fiddlers faced whichever way they chose: given audience members would see the fronts of *some* fiddlers. In any case, the accompanying guitars clustered close, and the prevailing view during a given performance was usually the back of one guitarist and sides of others (although, more recently, a film of the performer has been projected above the contest stage).

Five minutes were budgeted for each fiddler. Mounting the stage and having the mike raised or lowered took a few moments, and an introduction citing name, perhaps age, home, profession, and past championships about half a minute (the judges, sequestered in the school library, heard only the fiddling: one staff member's job was to turn the audio link on and off). Performances of three tunes—a breakdown, waltz, and tune of choice (often a rag)—fit into four minutes, and then the next fiddler was on deck. This seems like very little time, yet emcee and staff are so skilled and experienced that the overall feel is of careful efficiency rather than hurry.

The days (and nights) in the gym flow smoothly, even elegantly. Evenings, when more of us in the audience aren't fiddlers, feature more entertainment of various kinds sandwiched within the continuing competition. The repertoires one hears vary in compactness: what is played for the competition is pretty regimented. Evening entertainment offers more variety, and the campground jamming is the most free of all. Breakdowns dominate, but I heard a Norwegian-sounding tune that an adult participant had learned at a Scottish fiddle camp, quite a bit of orthodox modern Irish fiddling, some swing, some bluegrass (although banjos and mandolins have no place on this contest stage), and even some old-time bands in "Stickerville," the distant satellite campground the denizens of which attend regularly but rarely compete. By Saturday morning, all present are relieved to have part of a day free of competition. It's a celebration in advance of the climax: a barbecue, a smallish craft fair, and a delightful downtown parade mixing the local cars and floats typical of parades with fiddle-themed floats from all over. Then Saturday night arrives, and the fiddlers with the most cumulative points face off.

So, is this the largest American fiddle contest, the best American fiddle contest, a truly "national" contest? Should these questions address the total experience of the stay in Weiser versus in other fiddle towns, or just the competition proper? As far as what happens on stage goes, more hours of fiddling are carefully presented here, more tunes total (albeit in ruthlessly summary versions), and a more thorough evaluation of contestants takes place than anywhere else, especially at the top level. That each fiddler truly in contention for prizes plays several of his or her sets of three tunes in contrasting genres helps keep the judging balanced, as do the factors of blind judging (to the degree that judges aren't familiar with specific fiddlers' idiosyncratic playing styles) and an "Olympic" system of throwing out the high and low scores.

The laudable attempt to be fair to all fiddle styles by drawing judges from many regions has had results uneven both within any given year of the contest and over the years. There's just too much variety in North American fiddling to allow any truly balanced evaluation of apples versus oranges versus grits. One long-term struggle between styles has been informally resolved: in Weiser, one must play in one of the elaborate linear western styles to win. No matter how skilled fiddlers may be in a rhythm-oriented style (say, one of the southeastern old-time styles

heard in Galax or West Jefferson, or in French-Canadian fiddling), they stand little chance for prizes unless they are in one of the senior brackets. This is much
of the reason that the old-time players who camp in "Stickerville" seldom enter
the contest arena. Also, although Canadian style from, for example, Ontario is
exciting and linear, Canadian fiddlers at Weiser find that they score better if they
adopt some cognate of Texas style for this contest. Nevertheless, true Texas fiddlers
also tend to be at a disadvantage owing to the action of several subtle interlock-
ing factors. The Idaho, Washington, and, recently, California fiddlers that triumph
most frequently at Weiser play in a composite style that has absorbed much of the
Texas technique of melodic variation, and many of these western fiddlers honestly
feel that they play in Texas style; however, what I will somewhat simplistically call
Weiser style favors a pure, nearly classical tone over the rhythmic drive that the
best Texas fiddlers have, a drive accomplished partly through bowing attacks and
emphases that can sound like flaws of timbre to most judges here.

Of course, there's nothing wrong with having a large contest for northwestern
fiddling, and that's exactly how this event was billed in its early years. That same
regional focus prevails today, but it's no longer acknowledged. Yes, there have been
eras when true Texas-style players won, including isolated instances fairly recently,
but those recent winners have triumphed in an uphill battle. As a result, many of
the top fiddlers in the United States, that is, the best of the true Texas fiddlers, attend Weiser sporadically or not at all. The usual winners at Weiser do sound great
but don't quite seem like the Texas-style fiddlers that some of them believe they
are.

How do Galax and Weiser compare in terms of sheer numbers of musicians
present? If one could believe the registration lists for Galax, that would be the
largest contest, but those lists are dubious: many register for competition just so
they can camp in the area reserved for musicians; they don't compete. I'd say that
there are about as many musicians at Weiser as at Galax, though a larger percentage are fiddlers at Weiser. How about the factor of geographic draw? An informal
census of how many fiddlers come from more than a hundred miles from the contest site places Weiser firmly in the lead, though this results in part from the West
being relatively sparsely populated. What about the jamming environment, which
most fiddlers say is more important than the formal competition? Weeklong stays,
unified campgrounds, and shirt-sleeve temperatures all aid good jamming and are
all characteristic of both Weiser and Galax, as well as somewhat smaller contests
such as Clifftop. But Weiser is at a bit of a disadvantage because of frequent high
winds and blowing grit. Last, how about the issue of quality? There are a dozen
or so truly astonishing fiddlers at each of the giant contests; however, the highest
average quality of playing over the hours is not found at the weeklong events but

rather at a few elite small events, and especially at the medium-sized contest I will describe next.

America's Best Fiddling Per Capita: The Texas State Championship

Texas fiddling is the source of the modern contest fiddling that dominates American fiddle contests outside the Southeast, and the better Texas contests feature incredibly skilled and exciting fiddling. Variation of the repeated strains is at the maximum for what is considered traditional American fiddling. This variety in presentation of a strain explores melody and emphasizes harmony rather than being primarily rhythmic (as is true in the Southeast).

Hallettsville reposes midway between Houston and San Antonio, just south of the interstate joining those megalopolises. It's small, at well under three thousand people. Owing to substantial immigration of Czechs from 1870 to 1900, the Catholic presence is visible, particularly in the city's main architectural surprise, a rambling Knights of Columbus facility, which was financed bit by bit by the profits from this fiddle contest. Parking is west of the large hall, while camping rings the parking lot and fills fields on the northeast perimeter of the property. A covered area stretching from immediately south to well west of the hall houses a high-quality craft show and a generous jamming area, while the northern acres ring with the sounds of a carnival. A barbecue cook-off stretches along the southern boundary and also fills an acre or so due east of the buildings. This is quite a spectacle: some dedicated cooks use the usual sideways barrels as ovens, but many others employ larger, arcane fiery apparatuses mounted on customized towing rigs. The smells are mesmerizing. But the hall has its own kitchen and also sponsors a crawfish boil Friday evening. After that feast, there's a bluegrass and Cajun music concert, and Saturday night a country dance, with all events separately ticketed. In short, the Knights have assembled a varied and extremely profitable composite festival, all centered on this official state fiddle contest. Most of the city's annual cycle of tourist-attracting events—a wild game supper, a kolache fest (kolaches are Czech Danishes), the South Texas Polka and Sausage Fest, two state championship domino tournaments—take place in the KC Hall, but the fiddle-centered festival in late April is the biggest affair of the year, just as in Galax and Weiser.

The contest is relatively short, and the schedule of competition straightforward. But this contest is special because of the general high level of playing and the unmatched focus on a single style. There are three age-defined competition brackets, the Senior Division (aged sixty-five and up), the Freshman Division (under sixteen years old), and the Open Division. In addition, there's a bracket for out-of-staters, one for the guitar accompanists (competing exactly as such, not as soloists), and occasionally an amusing repertoire quiz. The first contestants, the seniors (twelve to fifteen of them, on average) begin playing early on Saturday (starting in 2006, on Friday night). They are the Texas fiddlers here who are least consistently in Texas style, partly because many started fiddling before Texas style fully coalesced. The Texas fiddlers' collective work ethic is certainly in place, however, and the overall quality of musicianship and technique is higher than among seniors at any other contest.

The Freshman Division has fifteen to twenty-five contestants, of whom blessedly few are Suzuki kids playing too soon in their learning curves. Instead, many of the young fiddlers belong to the studios of either Joey and Sherrie McKenzie of Burleson (in the Dallas-Fort Worth area) or Jimmie Don Bates of Austin, and these are very fine Texas fiddle studios, in both cases inspiring tremendous effort on the part of students. One family moved to be closer to the McKenzies so that the three daughters could study easily. And Jimmie Don doesn't have students from the Austin area only: a number who live in Texas drive five or more hours and must therefore structure some family weekends around taking a lesson. He has students coming in sporadically from as far away as Montana and even from Alaska. These are not cuddly teachers—Jimmie Don has a widespread reputation as an irascible perfectionist—but they get fine results.

Next comes the bracket for guitar accompanists, in which just one guitarist accompanies a fiddler rather then the usual three to five, and the mike focuses on the guitarist. Time permitting, the "Texas Jackpot" follows. (Time has not permitted the last few years; the contest is growing.) This is a comic test of breadth of repertoire, a round robin in which each competitor contributes a few dollars to the "jackpot" that the winner will take home. They draw tune titles from a hat, then either play the tune or pretend to, in which case a judge rings a cowbell or honks an air horn to eject them from the bracket. Last on Saturday afternoon, we hear the "Gone to Texas" bracket, named after a slogan left on cabin doors points east of Texas in the nineteenth century when the owners of the cabins immigrated to Texas. This out-of-state bracket is quite specifically defined; it is for Texas-style fiddlers (only) who have the misfortune of residing elsewhere. An average year sees twelve to twenty competitors from as close as Oklahoma (where true Texas style dominates), from New York, from Colorado, and from the Northwest axis. There is no competition Saturday evening, but the better fiddlers jam well into the morning in the campground and hotel rooms and, especially, at a massive party held at the home of the son of the founder of the contest.

Sunday morning's Hall of Fame Induction (discussed near the end of the next chapter), generates performances of about fifteen tunes. But the final Open Division is what everyone is waiting for. About twenty-five to thirty players start out with two tunes (one of which must be a breakdown), and then play a tune in one or another genre specified by the judges as the group narrows to twenty, to ten, and finally to three. The playoff of the final three is the most dramatic and musically strong event in the fiddle world. All three fiddlers stay on stage throughout this portion. The judges require that each of the three plays a breakdown, then a waltz, then a polka, then a rag, then a swing tune (the exact order in which the genres are specified varies from year to year, but it's these five genres). The tunes are mainstream tunes. Indeed, there are few enough preferred polkas that two of the three may play, say, "Clarinet Polka," and few enough rags that two fiddlers may play, for example, "Cotton Patch Rag." In any case, the confrontation is the most direct in the world of contest fiddling, the level of performance as high as or higher than anywhere else, and the choice of a winner can be agonizing.

Why is the playing level so high and the excitement so powerful? There's the tradition of excellence and the associated etiquette: few fiddlers enter unless they are good players, and this includes the kids, who study hard with their excellent teachers. Also, the repertoire commonly performed doesn't extend beyond a few dozen pieces in each genre. Any yearning for musical variety is satisfied by the complexity of the arrangements of pieces rather than choice of what is seen as raw material. That many individual fiddlers are personally involved in arranging tunes results in enhanced understanding, commitment, and musicianship. The limited repertoire also helps intensify the attention of the audience, because nonfiddlers are more likely to be able to recognize the tunes than at contests outside of Texas.

Last, what is the relationship between this and the "national" contest in Weiser? The top players at Weiser, that is, the top players in Washington/Idaho contest style, freely—indeed explicitly—acknowledge that they play in what is essentially Texas style. In fact, many northwestern fiddlers simply equate their style with Texas style, and many of them have lived in Texas and studied with Texans. Among these fiddle-motivated immigrants, the West-Coast-raised McKenzies are still here, as is Tonya Rast Hopkins, who moved to Texas as a college student, and the line between these immigrants' style and that of the environment to which they moved can become small to nonexistent. One of the principle models for northwestern players, Montana resident senior fiddler Dick Barrett, is from Texas and has remained a true Texas player. But, overall, one can hear a small but certain difference, a valuing of crystalline timbre at the expense of aggressive rhythm in the visitors' playing.

In 2001, Hallettsville's Gone to Texas bracket was briefly abandoned, with its constituency being fed into the open category, and a non-Texan was among the judges. If the outsiders could beat Texans at their own game, so be it. But the visitors did poorly. Some of them thought that there was epidemic bias in the judging (a novel complaint, since this contest has the lowest gripe quotient of any), and some of the Texas players felt that the outsiders had been put in their collective place. Cooler, more reflective heads opined that there was something about Texas playing that only Texans can do best. I'm not sure that distinction will hold forever; Alabamans Daniel Carwile, Mark Ralph, and Sharon Bounds are true Texas players and could do well in Hallettsville's Open Division. But the Idaho and Washington and other northwestern players, while playing in something extremely similar to Texas style, persist in going their own way. Both Hallettsville and Weiser will continue to claim to be the top fiddle contest in the nation. Weiser bases its claim for preeminence on its "national" name and on both sheer number of fiddlers and breadth of their geographic origin, plus the quality of the central bracket of competition. Hallettsville, where the prize money actually exceeds that at Weiser, counters with the facts that Texas is the source of contest-style fiddling and that Texas players both through inheritance and through talent and effort remain the very best Texas-style fiddlers.

CHAPTER THREE

Fiddle Contests Away from the Stage

E very successful fiddle contest is a multifaceted festival in which the formal competition serves as the anchor, sometimes one barely tolerated (as in Galax) but sometimes quite important (as in Weiser and Hallettsville). Still, every fiddler values other parts of the event more.

Location, Location, Location: Camping, Jamming, and Talking

Most participants in fiddle contests agree that jamming and catching up with old friends and making new ones are the most important aspects of these events. And, after all, a given fiddler is only standing on the stage and competing for a few minutes. A contest is unlikely to flourish without comfortable camping arrangements and convenient motels and without lots of space for informal playing. This need for generous room for various activities is a good part of the reason that most of the best fiddle contests take place in small towns, in which lots of parking is available every day.

Even the shortest of successful contests allow overnight stays. For instance, the Ashe County, North Carolina, contest takes place on a single Saturday, just from late afternoon until around midnight, but most participants camp anyway. Since the fiddle world is overall a blue-collar cultural complex, most participants sleep in recreational vehicles or campers pulled by pickups or SUVs rather than in the tents that urban fiddlers favor. Attendees who do not own or do not care to bring RVs or campers may stay in motels, but this is the exception. The dual musical makeup of this typical small southeastern contest—that is, that there are roughly as many old-time ensembles as bluegrass groups—is well served by the terrain of Ashe County Park. The larger RVs, many housing bluegrass groups, cluster in a flat area near the stage. Smaller campers and a few tents gather on a neighboring slightly hilly area; smaller old-time ensembles dominate there.

Although the organizers of many contests wish to place arriving campers in the next available spot in order to be efficient and avoid wasted space, musicians often have their own ideas about where they want to be, and especially whom they would like to be near. I already mentioned the miserable process this entails at the mammoth contest at Galax, Virginia. There's less of a systematic attempt to assemble camps in friendship groups at the "national" contest in Weiser Idaho; however, large complexes of tents and campers cluster in the outposts of the major fiddle studios of the Northwest, that is, the Ludikers of the Spokane, Washington, area, and the Hartz/Rast contingent of Meridian, Idaho. These two groups of fine fiddlers are friendly, and representatives teach at each others' summer camps, although they maintain a humor-laced but very real rivalry. In fact, a few years ago, when vehicle camping included Weiser High School's football field, the two studios always claimed the land around the respective goal posts.

While most of the fiddling at Weiser is in the northwestern substyle of Texas contest fiddling, the Northwest is also home to many urban revivalist old-time musicians. Although dozens of these revivalists attend Weiser, few compete or even to go to the gym to witness the competition. Instead, they camp on the northwest fringe of the permitted area and jam and socialize constantly. This area, nicknamed "Stickerville," constitutes a subculture at Weiser, a constellation of musicians and friends who absorb energy from the contest atmosphere; they meet *at* but independent of the contest. Because most of them are *urban* revivalists, the percentage of tents rises. Now, Weiser can get very breezy. In 2003, this affected the residents of Stickerville adversely. Brutal winds blew a port-a-can over and rolled it through campsite after campsite, flattening and dampening hi-tech and plebeian tents democratically.

Many contests are held outdoors, but with provisions made for continuing if the weather deteriorates. Weiser remains indoors, since there are so many entrants. The Texas state contest takes place inside too, and a few smaller ones book a high school auditorium or similar facility to avoid constructing a stage. But, just as small towns feel right for contests, sitting outdoors matches the flavor of the events best. The flyer advertising a given contest often includes the phrase "bring your lawn chairs," and, even when organizers set out ranks of folding chairs, veteran audience members haul out their own chairs and substitute them in. A nice lawn chair is not only comfortable, it's personal property, thus reserving a spot.

The holiday flavor of sitting outdoors to listen to music and of camping can exact a cost. The sun can be merciless. Many contests take place evenings only: at Galax, only the last day includes an afternoon portion. At smaller contests that include daytime events, audiences slowly relocate their fleets of chairs to follow the shade. Rain may cause a delay or a shift indoors, though sometimes audience members must choose between getting wet and leaving. The phrase "will take place rain or shine" in contest advertisements is both promise and threat! Soggy ground can impede navigation. Wind can be a problem when it whistles across microphones or, in far-from-rare, more extreme cases, when it outright assaults campers, as at Weiser. And cold restricts how late in the fall or early in the spring contests can be held outdoors in a given locale.

Food, Crafts, and Carnival

Fiddle contests are generic American festivals in the sense that food stands, a craft market, and, sometimes, supplementary nonmusical entertainment surround the stage, taking up several acres. The added activities suit both tradition and modern needs. On the historical side, this variety of attractions echoes venerable fiddling venues such as the county fair. Fiddle contests are longer than most concerts, and even the most dedicated audience members must eat eventually, and welcome something to do when they need a rest from the formidable series of very short performances that constitute a contest. What is most intriguing about the allied elements is that each mirrors the nature of the fiddling in a very general way, that is, in the mixing of traditional and modern ingredients. And food, crafts, and carnival also each draw on their own subcultures, ones partly overlapping with and partly independent of the fiddle world.

Food, food, and more food: it's plentiful, priced fairly reasonably, and available at stands set up within walking distance of the stage. It's usually fast food, although some offerings can be regionally distinctive or otherwise interesting. The nonregional, reliably standard component includes the usual sorts of meals served from a portable stand, that is, exactly what one eats at state and county fairs. These hot dogs, hamburgers, Italian and/or Polish sausage are traditional in two senses, in their long tenure as outdoor festival food, and, in a health-conscious age, their countless and yet uncounted calories (festivals are, after all, times away from dull responsibility). Other offerings have regional associations. For instance, the philanthropic organizations that run western North Carolina contests often maintain a booth at which burgers are outshone by North Carolina barbecue. Perhaps the *least* distinctive "regional" food at a contest that I've visited was in Weiser, Idaho.

The Elks booth honors the noble potato through supplementing their burgers and such with fries, chips, *and* hash browns throughout the day. In contrast, the Texas state contest offers regional food referencing three aspects of Hallettsville's geography. This small town, just a touch over one hundred miles west of Houston, is beef country. Second, this part of Texas is peopled by lots of descendants of immigrants from central Europe. And, third, it's just over an hour to the gulf coast. So there's a barbecue contest, Czech-style breakfast rolls (kolaches) for sale each morning, and a crawfish boil on Friday night.

A good half of the dozens of craft stands attached to most fiddle contests market country kitsch such as pot holders and wooden medallions and saws on which rustic sayings have been stitched or sewn or carved or burned: "Y'all Come Back!"; "Kissin' Don't Last—Cookin' Do"; "Bachelor Seeks Wife with Boat: Send Picture of Boat." Other products repose along the continuum from kitsch to craft, such as paintings of outdoor scenes, coat racks, and so forth.

To illustrate more interesting crafts in various categories, I'll draw on ones for sale at a small contest in Moulton, Alabama, in August of 2003. On the artistic end of the spectrum, Ray Dutton of near Moulton made elaborate birdhouses; woodworking is the commonest truly impressive craft regularly represented at fiddle contests and cognate festivals. At other fiddle contests, I've seen furniture in various states of finish, lathe-turned bowls of exotic woods, fancy wine bottle corks, carved staffs, and so forth, often made by retired or semiretired carpenters like Dutton. He stated that he could attend a festival within eighty miles of Moulton nearly every weekend during the warmer parts of the year. Other relatively high-level crafts include fancy pottery and poured concrete stepping stones decorated with stained glass patterns.

Other craftsmen sell not only their own relatively pricy work but also some less expensive items made elsewhere, often in foreign sweatshops. Howard and Judy Ryals, of near Montgomery, Alabama, make fancy leather belts, purses, and saddlebags but also cater to customers who want to spend less by offering leather wallets made in India. I've seen parallel casual mixes of classy homemade and cheaper imported goods many times. One man who visits Hallettsville some years makes birdfeeders in which examples of Depression glass bowls shade mason jars to which commercial chick feeders are attached, but also sells cheaper Chinese-made garden decor such as copper-wire dragonflies, turtles, and birds on wire stands.

A few stands are of types specific to fiddle contests and bluegrass festivals. Some are music stores' stands, stores that may be local (as was the case in Moulton) or from farther away. Stores that concentrate more on recordings may also be represented and again may be local or national (representatives of County Records show up at some of the larger contests). CDs offered may be of individual performers present at the festival, may concentrate fairly narrowly on one or several styles of fiddling or bluegrass, or may more generally offer country music, thus aiming less at fiddle aficionados than at locals who attend a contest because it's nearby and in some way congruent with rural tastes.

Fiddlers love to handle and discuss fiddles. Fiddle hobbyists whose enthusiasm has gotten out of hand may sell fiddles at contests. Generally, each hobbyist owns a large RV and transports his fiddle business in it, displaying his wares on folding tables in the shade offered by awnings unfurled from the RV. At Moulton, Jerry McGlocklin of Athens, Alabama, has a great time talking to the fiddlers trying out instruments and does sell enough to make it worth his while. Although he has been in the used car business all his working life, these fiddle weekends are as important to him as to the most avid fiddlers. While fiddles are generally sold by middlemen such as Jerry, high-quality fretted stringed instruments are marketed by their makers at a few contests. At Moulton, this category of craftsman was represented by Daniel Lewis, of Lafayette, Georgia, a younger guy who makes banjos and repairs various stringed instruments but specializes in historic-style banjos.

Figure 4. Jerry McGlocklin, selling fiddles and chatting with fiddlers in Athens, Alabama, 2003. He judges at that contest frequently and helps out in many ways.

Layers of Community: Family and "Family"

Harper Van Hoy, organizer and emcee of the large annual Fiddler's Grove Ole Time Fiddler's and Bluegrass Festival on his land near Union Grove, North Carolina, feels strongly about the importance of community and related values in the event to which he has devoted much of his life. In 1977, his emcee narration included these phrases:

> This is an educational festival, a family festival . . . This is our 73rd continuous festival
> since Daddy started the contest in 1924 to raise money for the schools . . . Fiddler's
> Grove is all about: it's teaching, it's sharing, it's learning, and it's fellowship and a
> good family atmosphere. And thank the Lord that he sends me such good people
> as you folks out there. . . . There's a certain continuity to this Fiddler's Grove event.
> Many families have come year after year after year. There's a family here tonight: Jim
> Dunn and his wife, whose son will be seven tomorrow, and he was here for the first
> time when he was thirty-six hours old.

With these words, Van Hoy allies this contest with quite a number of communities, that of the place (Fiddler's Grove as part of Union Grove), with his ardently felt Protestant Christianity, with a good cause (education), with family and the generations within families, with friends, and with historical continuities of community. While Van Hoy is unusually eloquent and explicit in expressing these values, each is important in the general flavor of fiddle contests.

Many contests demonstrate linkage with place through recruiting prominent citizens to welcome the audience to the event. Since nearly all fiddle contests take place in very small towns and since these events contribute significantly to the local economy while remaining family events, town mayors are delighted to give short speeches. At the Texas State Championships and Fiddlers Frolics, perennial emcee Harvey Norris always praises the host town of Hallettsville: "This is a little town of less than three thousand people, and by pulling together, they can put on a show like they do here."

Galax is on the large side among towns that host highly successful fiddle contests. Its population has stabilized at about seven thousand. At the weeklong "convention" in Galax, a modest amount of ceremony precedes the formal competition each night. Since many participants and audience members do not show up until later in the week, there needs to be a fresh introduction of the contest each evening. There's a crescendo in the status of celebrity speechifiers toward the busiest evenings of Friday and Saturday. On the first night, Monday night, the mayor of Galax welcomed us briefly, and we listened to an invocation and the national anthem before the scant few dozen of us in the audience heard kids play various instruments. Tuesday night, with a growing but still modest audience, the head of the Moose spoke, the mayor held forth again, a different minister blessed the event (this duty rotated through the leaders of the six largest white Protestant churches in town), and different musicians led "The Star-Spangled Banner." Finally, on Friday, all the stops came out, with a state senator, the lieutenant governor, and political candidates added to the mix, all ritually (but efficiently) extolling the contest's virtues: tradition, foot-tapping music, family values, and, not incidentally, economic stimulus to the region.

Most contests support good causes, ones with immediate local impact, generally through the agency of men's clubs mixing business with fellowship and good works. Helping in the area of education has been common for decades. At the 1990 Ashe County, North Carolina, contest (sponsored by the Rotary Club), the emcee reminded the audience that "all the funds, all the profits from this venture go back to our young people in our community. Usually, the last several years, we've donated a little over fifteen thousand dollars to high school scholarships, and that's every bit of the profit that's derived from this." The contest a few weeks later in nearby Fries, Virginia, supports the volunteer fire department, and another nearby contest in Sparta, North Carolina, supports local projects of the Lions Club. The bodies of contestants (much of the audiences) are nearly the same at these events; only the location and the good cause of the week vary. And it's not very different when a local chamber of commerce sponsors a contest, as in Weiser, Idaho; the cast of characters is much the same as in the philanthropic men's clubs, and the main financial benefit is the same, that is, bringing a flood of customers to local stores, restaurants, and motels.

Another part of the social fabric supporting—and to a degree supported by—fiddle contests is the religious establishment. Just as ministers in Galax were systematically tapped to give invocations on the various nights of that long event, shorter contests spread this duty (and church advertisement) among local church leaders over the course of years, since they have just one or two invocations per contest. At Fiddler's Grove, Harper Van Hoy invites a local minister to open Saturday night of the festival with prayer, but on Friday gives thanks himself to "Jesus for beautiful weather, [for bringing] wonderful people to us to listen to the music these musicians have learned and which has been passed on down to them, and they're passing their music on to the coming generation" (1997 phrasing).

Another way religion infuses these contests is through song. In bluegrass, particularly in the Southeast, gospel numbers figure large in many ensembles' repertoires. In contests, a group generally plays two tunes, often selected to contrast and thus show off what a band can do even in tightly restricted time. In many places in the country, bands seeking that breadth of presentation play one purely instrumental piece to show the virtuosity of each band member and also one vocal number. In the Southeast, many bands perform two pieces with vocals, one being a gospel number. In fact, there are a fair number of bluegrass bands that only play gospel. And in the "Song" or "Folksong" division of many southeastern contests, many songs are sacred.

I'll turn now to the ubiquitous term "family." Most fiddlers characterize the whole fiddle community as a family, and many an emcee describes a contest as family entertainment. Fiddle contests nurture both an enormous figurative family and an endless series of real families. In the Wallace family of Alvarado, Texas, Brooke, the eldest of six Wallace children, became intrigued by fiddling after seeing a hillbilly action figure in a computer game, then eventually studied fiddle with master Texas fiddler and teacher Jimmie Don Bates. But while Brooke's entry into the fiddle world began on the outside, each of her siblings started because fiddling was now in the family. When Brooke competes, her father, Paul, plays guitar, and when her younger brothers and sisters compete, Brooke accompanies too on tenor guitar. Many younger fiddlers are accompanied on stage by a parent or a teacher playing guitar during the solo competition, and many old-time bands and bluegrass bands are made up largely or exclusively of family members. Despite the level of commitment required of the whole family in terms of sheer hours and of the family calendar, many parents welcome and cultivate their kids' interest in fiddling. They do so because they believe that participation in this wholesome social complex will help keep their kids from becoming involved in less salubrious activities and will develop good self-discipline and other healthy mental habits. The fiddle world does tend to fill all of what otherwise might have been free time, so it comes as no surprise that many romances, indeed marriages, develop within it. And deep friendships result too within age and gender groups. At many a contest, a fine young fiddler will come back on stage to compete just after accompanying a friend, with that same buddy is now playing guitar.

Fiddling spans the generations in an era when not much else does. Children (and grandchildren) who likely live separately from their elder relatives, and may harbor contrasting political views and different tastes in many areas, nevertheless learn avidly from those elders' fiddling. Having contests divided into brackets by age doesn't just give the novice and the formerly agile their own protected chances to shine on stage. It's in those "outer" brackets that the announcer at many contests specifies not just where fiddlers are from but how old they are. And the very youngest and oldest fiddlers receive wild applause on that account, however tentative their playing still is or how shaky it has become. At some contests, there will be a moment when the youngest and the oldest fiddler are asked to stand on stage side by side for our cheers; I've seen a fiddler aged three or four up there together with a man in his nineties more than once. In addition, an excellent senior fiddler may be singled out for praise in a separate ceremony rather like the lifetime achievement award at the Oscars.

The most fully developed ceremony of homage I have seen is that at the Texas state contest in Hallettsville, in the annual induction of a fiddler (or other major figure in the contest system) into the Texas State Contest Fiddlers Frolics Hall of Fame. The hall of fame itself is a photographic gallery (with small newspaper article and other informational archive) housed in a room off of the main hall at the Knights of Columbus facility in Hallettsville, a room open throughout the contest. The 2000 ceremony, which occupied an hour and a half on Sunday morning, consisted of the reading of a short biography of inductee Dale Morris by emcee Harvey Norris. The narrative followed Morris from his youth through his early training on several instruments to his discovery of Texas fiddling when he was invited to jam with Texas fiddle greats at the age of eighteen. Then Norris described Morris's career as a fiddler in a number of important western swing and country bands, as a member of Bill Monroe's Bluegrass Boys, and as the operator of a prominent fiddle studio. A subsequent parade of praise and performances from students and friends had a bit of the flavor of a roast. Each speaker said something about Morris; then those who were fiddlers played a tune—one that they had learned from him, or that he had written, or that they associated with him for any other reason. These speakers praised him for his patience, kindness, lack of ego, and influence through many students, boldness in exploring repertoire, and so forth. Ricky Turpin, several times state champion himself, remarked that Morris was a fine example of the Tommy Jackson school of playing (Jackson fiddled in the band backing singer Ray Price). Turpin went on to compliment Morris on his composition of "lots of pretty waltzes. I think every time he got married, he wrote a pretty waltz."

With Turpin's deft comic detour, we enter the "roast" aspect of the hall of fame induction. By recalling Morris's bon mots and practical jokes, and adding their own witticisms, a dozen speakers helped portray him as a prominent exponent of the rascally side of fiddling, an aspect absolutely central in Texas. One speaker had noticed Dale wearing sunglasses one Sunday morning and asked how he had slept. The answer: "I went to bed at 6:45. I got up at a quarter to seven." Jimmie Don Bates pointed out the rift between the family-oriented contest environment and the specifically male part of the fiddle world, one full of testosterone- and alcohol-fueled exuberant misbehavior: "I had a story to tell, but since this is not a roomful of drinking men, I think I'll skip it." But guitarist Bobby Crispin ignored that gap: "I've known Dale for thirty-one, thirty-two years. We've been through a lot together, and there's a lot of it I can't tell. . . . In fact, most of it I can't tell. . . . I really can't think of *anything* I can tell." But then, having softened us up, he continued: "We went to a contest in Langley, Oklahoma, and they had a little old motel there that would hold about thirteen or fourteen people. So we all'd rented this room, and all went to sleep, bunked here and there. Dale got in late one time, and he just thought how funny it would be to pull a little joke. So he rounded up a bunch of cats, and put them in his car. And he stopped at the store and got about a half pound of bologna. He herded all those cats in the door so they couldn't get out, then he went around and laid a piece of bologna on everybody's chest. In a little while was the payoff." When Wes Westmoreland's turn to honor Morris arrived he began his speech by responding to that story briefly: "I was in Langley, and I peeled bologna off me for thirty minutes." And with these anecdotes, we move to the next topic.

Humor

Humor on many levels helps set the overall mood and leavens the tension of competition at most fiddle contests. Much of the humor lies in the music itself. Cunning syncopations and other purely sonic wit abounds, and many tunes' titles have wry or slapstick flavor ("Whiskey before Breakfast," "Who Comes in When I Go Out?" and so on). Contestants will throw in a short joke now and then, and every emcee inserts a few fairly wholesome jokes to paper over delays occasioned by weather, slow stage changes, and so forth. For instance, in Hallettsville in 2002, a judge's need to hold up the contest for a minute to visit the bathroom prompted the emcee to follow suit, in itself mildly amusing. Then that emcee linked the serial micturation with a joke: "Randy [Elmore, a judge] came by here, and all of a sudden I had to do the same thing Randy was doing, and I said it must be catching. And it reminded me of a story of a little boy in school. He had to go to the bathroom. And when he got back the teacher said 'Johnny, did you wash your hands?' and he said 'Nope.' And she said 'Didn't your parents teach you to wash your hands?' And he said 'Nope.' 'Didn't they teach you anything at all?' He said 'Yep.' 'What did they teach you?' 'They taught me not to pee on my hands.'"

In all of these small ways, humor permeates every contest. And it is this continuous stream of humor in the music, in the tune titles, and in the talking on stage that is clearly the most important aspect of humor at these events. But humor as a leavening agent is so critical that many contests feature additional more formal and extended mechanisms meant as amusing departures from the contest proper. For instance, in the 1997 contest in Mount Airy, North Carolina, the adult buck dancers eschewed the usual serious approach. Instead, many dancers executed a variety of comic moves, and a fair number also sported bizarre costumes, for instance, one aping Barney, the irritatingly wholesome purple dinosaur in a children's television show.

The Texas state contest has a unique bracket called the Texas Jackpot, which tests contestants' breadth of repertoire. Judges draw tune titles from a hat, and fiddlers either play the tune or, if they don't know that one, fake it. Errors are rewarded with the sound of a cowbell or air horn. This bracket is a genuine test of knowledge and tends to be won by the most fluent fiddlers. This contradicts a complaint heard at many contests that winners know just a few tunes that they have polished obsessively for the occasion. The champions in Hallettsville clearly know plenty of tunes, even though they choose from a tiny subset for the competition proper.

There's precious little time to chuckle during the competition at the enormous and efficiently run contest in Weiser, Idaho, though a few funny moments sneak in anyway. In 2001, a senior fiddler told the audience that she had "paid off the judges." Such moments, however, are rare, and the general texture of this contest remains dead serious. But the one deliberately funny competition bracket is just as carefully developed as the main brackets of the contest. Each evening, a few "certified" fiddlers, that is, fiddlers who have won a given age-defined competition bracket at a contest "certified" as worthy by the authorities at Weiser, are invited to play anything they want for three minutes or so. Such performers generally try to be funny. The majority don a costume and/or perform rudimentary theatrics corresponding to a given tune's title. In 2001, one fiddler dragged an extra bow to the stage (on the floor, with a rope) before playing "Dragging the Bow," and another played "Back Up and Push" while doing that to his accompanist. Another presented "Turkey in the Straw" as an old-fashioned frolic song with the audience echoing "Haw Haw Haw" at the appropriate spot in the chorus, and another fiddler played that same tune while encased in what must have been a very warm turkey suit. Yet another inspired effort featured the performing family's pet dog on stage howling at climactic moments. But the very best act in the "certified" division was more complex. Two very short brothers, Alex and Hayden Duncan, who do very well in the most junior branches of formal competition at Weiser, teamed up to sing and play a version of "El Paso," a well-known epic country song in which a cowboy infatuated with a barroom girl named "Felina" shoots a man, leaves, then must try to return to her, despite the inevitability of his own demise. These tiny boys wore ponchos too big for them, and sang this lugubrious text with

Figure 5. One evening at Weiser in 2001, the Duncan brothers played a sad country song in a hilarious manner.

utmost sincerity, but with piping little voices. One of the boys' mariachi-style fiddled answers to the pair's vocal phrases were just slightly exaggerated in style, and the whole package was hilarious.

As a final illustration of the systematic airing of rough, rural humor at fiddle contests, I'll return to Mississippi. Although the state contest for Mississippi is weak overall, the humor component stands out. This is, after all, formally entitled the Mississippi State Fiddlers and Liars Contest. In an average year, four to six humorous tall tales appear singly between the divisions of music competition. Some of these extended narratives explore modern topics in rough-edged ways. One joke in the 2002 contest consisted of an extended pun satirizing the veterinary profession. In brief, a widow transported her comatose German shepherd to the veterinarian. Was there any hope? The vet brought in two animal diagnosticians, a black Labrador retriever, which sniffed the supine dog and detected no signs of life, and a cat that looked at it with the same lack of results. The vet justified his astronomical bill to the outraged widow as follows: "He had a lab test and a cat scan." But most of the jokes evoke rural history and inherited attitudes much as fiddle tunes do. Jokes must be family-friendly and politically and religiously neutral, though making fun of intellectuals is certainly OK.

Wayne Carter (liar #3 in 2002), told this tale:

> The story I want to tell you about, it's—a lot of you older folks can identify with me on this—it happened a long time ago, 1950. I was six years old. And we were share-

croppers, so we weren't rich—you know about the sharecroppers? We lived over in the northeast part of the state, in Monroe County, right there next to the Alabama line. And we didn't have running water in the house. We didn't have electricity, so no telephone, no television. And we didn't have a refrigerator. We'd have to go to the ice plant and get a hundred-pound block of ice, you know, and it'd keep about five or six days if you kept it insulated real good. The neighbors were something special back then. If you had a problem, they would come and help you, no question about it: they were going to help you.

But this particular day was on a Saturday. It was coming up a bad weather, coming out of the south. And about three families had walked across the field to sit the storm out with us. And all of the grownups had taken all of the chairs. We had those little straight-legged split-bottomed chairs—you know what I'm talking about. Me and my brother, we just sit on the floor with our duck-head overalls on, right down on the floor. And they were sitting around the old radio listening to the [news about] storm. It was severe—thunder, tornadoes, damaging hail, and lightning. And they were all sitting with their heads down listening to the weather.

And I jumped up and said "Grandmother . . . (she raised me—I called her Grandma—my mother died when we were real young, so my grandmother—she loved us kids, and she raised us) . . . Grandma, I've got to go to the bathroom." There was a simple old toilet, and it sit about 125 yards away from the house. But I run out through the back door, and off of the steps. I didn't touch the steps, I just left the floor and went right out on the ground about eight feet away from the house and hit running down the path right down to the toilet. It had a big . . . the whole front of it opened up into a door. So I ran in down there and I got up in there on the little chair.

And I had done finished everything, and I was just sitting there listening to the hail. And the rain—it began to get close, you know. I could hear the rain beat up on that old toilet. The wind gusted up about sixty or seventy miles an hour and blew the thing right over on its face, right over on the door! And I tell you, I was scrambling around there, and I just *thought* I had finished. And I got my overalls hooked around one gallus, and I began to try to find a way out of that thing. Well, the only way out was down through the hole! And I could get my head through there, but I couldn't get my shoulders through there, even though I didn't weight fifty pounds. Well, I backed up, and I was beginning to get a little scared, and I reached in and grabbed a hold of a little board. And I began to pull it. And I could hear the nail squeaking, coming loose. So I really put out, and I jerked the board plum off. I got down through the hole then.

To get out, I had to get across about a four-foot pit. And you know what that is: that's a septic tank. And I knew the storm was right on me, so I revved up with one foot, and I gave it all I had, barefooted (we went barefooted almost year 'round).

And so I landed right on the outside of that old pit. And, being wet and barefooted, I slipped, and I rolled down in there waist deep. Well, that scared me the most! I come out of there, and up that trail I went. I mean, I was gittin' it, and I could run! If I could get a step ahead, you couldn't catch me. And I run up to the front door of the house and into the living room I went, right up there amongst them. They was still sitting around there with their heads down when I run up. My grandmother said "Son, you didn't make it, did you?" I said, "Yes Ma'am, Grandma, I made it. In fact, I made it about as far down that toilet as you can go!"

In brief, humor matters because the atmosphere of the contest is so absolutely critical. Constant returns to witty music, to wry sayings, to G-rated and good-hearted jokes, even to the slapstick of special contest brackets, help set an optimistic, low-key, and overall pleasurable tone. This is the way we want to remember we have been, and would like to believe we can be.

Nostalgia

Why do so many musicians keep coming to fiddle contests year after year, even the big ones with all their physical inconveniences? That they choose to negotiate the inevitable irritations of even Galax is a vivid and annually reinforced testimony to both the enduring appeal of the music and the values associated with old-time music and bluegrass, namely doing something for yourself, communion with family and friends, and faith that a "better" past can be invoked to shape a healthier present and future. Each of these levels of values matters greatly. In interviews, when I asked fiddlers why they fiddled, their replies often started with the phrase "to do something for myself." But, while the solo efforts required to attain competence as a fiddler have individual rewards in terms of shaping character and personal satisfaction, this work must be accomplished within layers of contacts, both in the ensembles in which fiddlers perform and in the immediate fact and extended feel of "family." That is, the health of the fiddle world ought never be evaluated *solely* in terms of abstract musical quality. It thrives through symbolizing the restoration of networks of human contact that have been frayed by modernity, both the fractured family and the threatened atmosphere of small-town life. It's true that many traditional musicians, especially those who play in old-time styles, live in what today pass for small towns. But the fact that these communities produce modest statistics in censuses and retain the visual texture of small towns (houses with generous yards with fields or forests nearby), can't guarantee the small-town *feel* of the past. Even the least of today's towns possess or are in easy range of a Wal-Mart, are linked by physical roads much easier to traverse than in past generations, and are joined with as much of the world as desired through satellite dishes and through the internet. Few traditional musicians would advocate backing away from these modern conveniences, but these changes cannot help but add to the friction between the ideal of the small town and the intrusive reality of the world at large.

Small towns physically represent nostalgia, that longing for an artificially rosy past that has long permeated the American psyche. The feel of dislocation that inspires nostalgia, while certainly not unique to the United States, has been intense here and always a central ingredient in entertainment. It is no accident that Charles Hamm's definitive history of American popular song is entitled *Yesterdays* (1979). For musicians who play at fiddle contests, nostalgia is not just a vague feeling but an emotional model made concrete on fiddle contest weekends and served especially well by the block of up to a week taken up by the grueling largest contests. It's not just abstract, general nostalgia then; it's a way of life briefly but intensely enacted.

"Nostalgia" is certainly a loaded term. *Webster's Dictionary* notes that it used to be defined as "a severe melancholia due to protracted absence from home or native place" (Gove 1971, 1542) and similar definitions have abounded in the world of medicine since the term was coined by Swiss doctor Johannes Hafer in 1688 (Boym 2001, 3). But "modern" nostalgia is something less harmful, an imaginative exercise bringing pleasant and poignant aspects of the past into the present. After all, nostalgia paints the past much as hope does the future, partly through logic and partly through desire. And nostalgia *supports* hope: if we believe that there really were "good old days," then there's a symmetrical possibility that the future can be more rational, more supportable, just plain better than the often confusing and alienating present. And so our yearning for those good old days recasts those earlier times as better than they ever could have been. To "live" nostalgia in a festival setting is certainly not hard. We simply focus on recalling and reifying the cherished parts of reimagined history. Any less desirable aspects can, just as simply, *not* be targeted by memory and action. I would like to go through how this works fairly systematically and to begin with the conceptually easiest sides of a festival. The most important thing to remember is that even though history forms the raw material for nostalgia, it is nostalgia that is being enacted at fiddle contests, not history.

Camping creates a cluster of dwellings roughly equal in size and quality, an egalitarian temporary village. And access to like-minded neighbors is easier than in the good old days. The neighbors are guaranteed to be like-minded, since they are present for the same purpose: to enjoy a given kind of music in a convivial setting. And the neighbors are close by. In the old days, one might walk across a hill or so to get to a friendly neighbor; the distance, while modest, was irreducible, since agriculture requires room. In the festival, next door is a matter of feet rather than miles. Also, when you encounter your neighbor, you automatically have time to spend together.

Being closer to nature through staging events outdoors gives a flavor of the past. Even the mild inconveniences of overly bright sun or chilly evenings can tweak memory favorably. But in inclement weather, one can move most events indoors or move oneself to the RV. Food connects with nature here, since regional stamps on food issue from local agriculture or availability of gathered foods such as fish or wild rice. Crafts may follow a similar regional pattern when they are made from locally available raw materials such as certain woods, local caches of clay, and so forth. Of course, both foodways and crafts follow region in cultural ways too, and tradition retains patterns even when nature runs out of materials (for instance, central North Carolina built a pottery tradition owing to initial availability of clay, but the potters' community outgrew that local supply long ago and imports clay now). Another factor reinforcing the nostalgic flavor of crafts is that crafts represent excellence in an egalitarian frame. Items are handmade by individuals, like in the old days. The range of items sold at a festival could *conceivably* be made by the visitors to the festival, and price ranges match the pocketbooks of the audience. And the broad range of items for sale fits tradition, for instance, furniture is always in some variation of country style rather than appearing remotely modern.

Even if earlier times were not truly simpler than today in terms of human relationships, reliving those times can be. In fiddle contests, we are all mild-mannered and unspecific Protestants (even the non-Protestants present). No one protests when there's an invocation, and the invocation will contain nothing divisive. And the occasional religious song is similarly nonsectarian.

Issues of race simply don't come up at fiddle contests. This is a largely blue-collar and almost entirely white world. The music contains strong African American influences, but few blacks have any affection for it today. There are no administrative or physical barriers to blacks attending fiddle contests, of course, and the rare black contestant will get just a bit more applause than his or her performance merits (I base this on a miniscule sample of black participants, including one urban-revival banjoist, a guitarist, a few Suzuki-trained novice fiddlers, one "liar," and two dancers in my decades of attending contests). The only African American in the audience during the years I attended the Ashe County, North Carolina, contest was a family retainer shepherding an affluent, frail, older white couple. That blacks choose to pass such events by was especially noticeable at this contest. Much of the city's small black population lives on the short road to the park, and numerous outdoor parties on contest evenings make their not coming to the contest seem a public statement, whether or not this was intended. But it has been only a few decades since nearby Mount Jefferson acquired that name, displacing the title Nigger Mountain. Blacks have much less reason than whites to idealize past rural life, to celebrate the "old days" in fiddle contests or in any other way; indeed, a much lower percentage of blacks than whites who live in small towns today do so by choice. Black fiddlers were common and influential *before* the current revival but are extremely rare today, and black families, having no stake in the particular brand of nostalgia lived at fiddle contests, simply feel no urge to attend.[1]

That blacks just aren't interested can be seen even more easily at contests held in urban settings. For instance, the Mississippi State Fair draws as many blacks as whites, and everybody at the fair walks within a few feet of the open structure housing the fiddle contest sooner or later, but only white passersby walk in and sit down. The same holds at the Tuscaloosa, Alabama, contest, held in the food court of a shopping mall patronized equally by blacks and whites. Blacks eating in the food court sit far away from the music without any tension being evident. Similar examples abound. Now, Native Americans participate in fiddling in large numbers in, for example, parts of Oklahoma, but it is clear that they are expressing the rural and assimilated layers of their identities when they fiddle. Last, while Latinos may attend festivities corollary to certain contests, they rarely hang around for the music. I quizzed some Mexicans and Mexican-Americans in Weiser during the Saturday morning parade. Did they like the music coming from those floats that featured fiddlers? Sure (I will conflate their replies) but not enough to drive to the high school and pay to hear it: they'd rather tune in to their own music, to norteña and ranchera and romantica on one of several Spanish-language channels on the radio.

Fiddlers and friends are generous with one another, as they would like to remember themselves having been in the good old days. What is new is that the impulse to share, for example, food is now generally supported by the ability to do so. "Family" can be more unified than actual family, the membership of which can be potluck. A common interest is now guaranteed, and relief from some temporary neighbor's occasionally grating habit is in sight, since the fiddle world consists of weekends. Friendship with older folks is, on the average, less problematic than in

---

1. Perhaps the most elegantly worded assessment of nostalgia was by a black writer, Ralph Ellison: "That which we remember is, more often than not, that which we would like to have been; or that which we hope to be. thus our memory and our identity are ever at odds; our history even a tall tale told by inattentive idealists." These phrases begin his article "The Golden Age, Time Past," which reassesses memories of the early years of jazz (1964, 199).

the real world, because the old folks at fiddle contests are easy to visit with since they are mobile and mentally vigorous, and the fact that the fiddling is tradition-oriented means that older fiddlers get an initial leg up in respect simply because of their age. Above all, fiddling provides a platform for communication in and beyond words, a flexible and delightful common ground.

CHAPTER FOUR

Fiddlers across the South

This chapter offers a picture of the collective backgrounds, activities, and tastes of today's fiddlers by synthesizing and excerpting interviews (four nearly complete interviews are transcribed in an appendix). I've been attending fiddle contests for most of my adult life but just started extensive formal interviewing for this book. The questions I regularly asked emerged from my broad but unsystematic past experience; the point of doing parallel interviews was to elicit and compare patterns of thought and behavior systematically. The main interview questions constitute the subheadings in this chapter. Thirty-one fiddlers interviewed are listed in tables 1 and 2. I grouped them according to their styles of fiddling, though the categories overlap. For instance, although the senior fiddlers constitute a coherent group as such, they could have been just as logically parceled out into the geographical listing, putting E. J. Hopkins with the Texas fiddlers and so forth. Also, fiddling in the West overlaps with urban revivalism both in terms of the high socioeconomic backgrounds of many fiddlers and in that many fiddlers in both groups started fiddling as adults. Pete Rolland, for example, is as much "urban revivalist" as from the West.

The arrangement of categories in the tables follows relationships between regional styles. The old-time, blackface-minstrel-derived styles of the Virginia/ North Carolina/Tennessee Appalachian area and of West Virginia are related, though that of West Virginia is what fiddlers call "notier," that is, more linear, with fewer immediate repetitions of given pitches (explored in chapter 5). Urban revivalists generally play in one or another old-time style, and bluegrass, though varied and often chromatic in a jazzy way, issues historically more from old-time fiddling than from contest style fiddling (with dramatic exceptions, such as contest champion and bluegrass fiddler Byron Berline). In table 2 Texas contest style comes first, since the other contest styles are oriented toward it. Contest fiddlers in the West

Table 1. Biographical Data for Interviewed Fiddlers Who Play in Older Styles or Bluegrass

Category of fiddler	Name	Date and place of birth/ residence	Father's profession	Fiddler's profession
Senior fiddlers from many places	Senator George Cecil McLeod	1927; SE MS; near birthplace	farmer, logger, school teacher	raises cattle, former state senator
	Roy Crawford	1934; AL	farmer	data processor
	Mack Snoderly	1937; TN; NC	farmer	dentist (retired)
	Kenny Sidle	1931; OH	millwright	millwright (retired)
	Bill Birchfield	1935; east TN	farmer, etc.	car repairs, salvage
	E. J. Hopkins	1929; near Ft. Worth; Houston	farmer, county commissioner	machinist, then police officer (retired)
Old-time, corner of Virginia, North Carolina, and Tennessee	Richard Bowman	1953; VA	tobacco farmer	farmer, musician
	Brian Grim	1970; b. PA, quickly to VA	carpenter	mailman, shearer, and fiddle teacher
	Rita Scott	Ashe County, NC	school teacher; mother secretary	scans photos for small publisher
	Tim Donley	1972; MD, then VA, now NC	science teacher, watch repairman	violin shop: maker, teacher, and fiddler
Old-time, West Virginia	Bobby Taylor	1953; WV	machinist for tractor company	librarian, archives/history library
	Jake Krack	1985; IN, to WV for fiddling	stonemason, music shop	student, perhaps to be chemist in W VA
Old-time, with revivalist element	Betty Vornbrock	1954; SD, IA to WV, TX, WV	psychiatric social worker	makes upholstered instrument cases
	Jim Cauthen	1947; AL	state highway department (both)	computer engineer for IBM
Bluegrass	Bill Rogers	1962; S MS, near birthplace	farmer	public health environmentalist
	Paul Shelasky	1951; NY to CA	violinist	bluegrass fiddler

Table 2. Biographical Data for Interviewed Fiddlers Who Play in Contest-Oriented Styles

Category of fiddler	Name	Date and place of birth/residence	Father's profession	Fiddler's profession
Texas	Ricky Turpin	1964; Lubbock, then Austin area	car business; mother a beautician	freelance musician
	Jimmie Don Bates	1964; East Texas, now Austin	career military, then construction	fiddle teacher and session musician
	Carl Hopkins	1959; most of life in Houston area	machinist, then police officer	welder
	Wes Westmoreland	1962; near Ft. Worth; Temple	road grader	fiddler in swing band, now pharmacist
(Idaho before; now Texas)	Tonya Hopkins	1968; ID, then Houston (w/ Carl)	fish hatchery; mother a teacher	fiddle teacher and school teacher
Idaho and the West	Tony Ludiker	1962; several moves; Spokane	brick plant	fiddle teacher and music store
	Mabel Vogt	1942; ID	logger and sawmill	adjunct German professor
	Starr McMullen	1951; NY, CA, OR	sales; mother with phone company	economics professor
	Pete Rolland	1946; IL, NY, AZ	violin professor	fiddler, music shop
	Amanda Kerr	1988; Alaska	researcher; mother a graphic artist	student
Tennessee Valley	Daniel Carwile	1973; Athens AL, now Nashville TN	barber	fiddle teacher and fiddler
	Mark Ralph	1963; KY to AL	school principal; mother a lab technician	dentist
	Lark Reynolds	1970; KY	police officer	health surveillance and fiddle contest organizer
	Joel Whittinghill	1973; KY	police officer	fiddle teacher, then account manager
	Sharon Bounds	1964; AL	coal miner	before marriage in bank, now home

and in the Tennessee Valley often believe that they play in Texas style, but close listening reveals differences (again, see the next chapter). Last, the senior fiddlers are more old-fashioned in style than the younger fiddlers. In a mild paradox, each senior fiddler's "older" playing is less stylistically homogenous than that of younger fiddlers in the same styles. Since the seniors inherited their styles as much as chose them, and since they also inherited the eclectic attitudes of fiddlers of the 1920s through the 1940s along with their repertoires, they play in styles relatively difficult to characterize in a few phrases.

"When and where were you born? Where have you lived? Your parents?"

These days, the fiddlers who triumph at major contests are generally in their twenties or thirties or, at most, early forties. Tony Ludiker, in his early forties as of this writing, has won the prestigious "national" contest at Weiser, Idaho, many times, but now considers himself as at an age-related disadvantage. The oldest fiddlers I interviewed do still compete, but they come into their own *off* the stage, in campground jamming. Indeed, although jams centered on the musical pyrotechnics of on-the-make kids or on the virtuosity of current champions are exciting, not as many tape recorders materialize as when the senior fiddlers hold forth. I remember an evening at Weiser when about thirty of us gathered around Dick Barrett, an elderly Texas fiddler now residing in Montana who has been a main source for the northwestern take on Texas fiddling. As he tuned, I discretely readied and positioned a tape recorder . . . as did nearly everyone else present. Somehow, an action that can be unobtrusive when one person does it loses its subtlety when part of a group ballet. Barrett politely ignored the machines. Their unveiling was no surprise but rather a regular ritual of respect and exercise of influence.

Among the younger generation of champion fiddlers, quite a few have managed to carve out livelihoods that are partly or wholly based on fiddling. Do their patterns of residence have anything to do with their paid fiddling jobs? Few of these musicians have been willing to move away from the style area of their fiddling. In fact, a fair number of fiddlers have relocated to be near the fiddling that they love the most. For instance, teenager Jake Krack's family moved from Indiana to West Virginia because they had been spending enormous amounts of time there for Jake to learn from venerable fiddler Melvin Wine. In a similar case, fiddling became so important in the young lives of the Quebe sisters (aged ten, thirteen, and fifteen in June of 2001) that the whole family moved within Texas to be closer to their teachers, Joey and Sherry McKenzie, who themselves had moved from the

Northwest to Texas to be able to earn a living as teachers of Texas-style contest fiddling. Related examples abound. Tonya Hopkins (at that time Tonya Rast) moved from Idaho to Texas to go to college, with the exact location (Houston) chosen to be close to Texas fiddlers her own age whom she'd met in Weiser. Among them was Carl Hopkins, whom she married. Her younger sister, Roberta Rast, recently moved to Texas too. Her decision to study violin at the University of Texas was linked to wanting to study fiddling with Austin resident and famous Texas fiddle teacher Jimmie Don Bates. Amanda Kerr, an enthusiastic teenage fiddler who has always lived in Anchorage, Alaska, plans in a general way to do the same thing: "I'm just a kid, so I'm still stuck here with family and friends. When I grow up, I plan to move somewhere where I can hear more of the music that I love."

"What's your profession? Your parents'?"

Most skilled fiddlers from anywhere but the West (and the category of revivalists) come from the middle of our socioeconomic spectrum, either from upper blue-collar backgrounds or the lower economic range of the white-collar world. Most of the parents of today's best fiddlers—many of those fathers fiddled too—are or were people who often didn't have an upper-level formal education or earn a great deal but had responsible jobs, ones in which care had to be taken, hard work done without a supervisor nearby, and independent decisions made. This would naturally produce an atmosphere at home conducive to learning fiddling, an enthusiasm involving lots of hard work, probing thought, and solitary practice. I should also note that many fiddlers and their parents have outdoor jobs or outdoor enthusiasms such as hunting and fishing, another echo of tradition in their lives.

Another category of fiddlers' professions issues naturally from the first. Children of upper-level blue collar workers who have been sent to college, that is, fiddlers who represent the first generation to get past high school, may end up in the lower reaches of the white collar world while retaining attitudes toward culture that issue naturally from those of their less-educated parents. A fair number of today's fine fiddlers are schoolteachers or have jobs in the lower rungs of the medical area. These patterns of fiddlers' and their parents' professions do not hold, however, when tradition has been interrupted, as in the case of urban revivalists and often in the case of fiddlers who live in the West. In these two groups, highly educated individuals lacking fiddling in the family or immediate neighborhood take up fiddling partly to express liberal ideology. In the East (and often elsewhere) such fiddlers are old-time purists with a special taste for especially exotic old-time tunes (true of both Betty Vornbrock and Jim Cauthen). In the West, while some revivalist fiddlers remain attached to old-timey style, others take up the Idaho school of Texas playing. In our sample, highly educated fiddlers with interrupted traditions include Starr McMullen (Ph.D. in economics), Pete Rolland (Ph.D. in mathematics), and Mabel Vogt (university adjunct professor of German).

Most of today's top fiddlers make a little money off of fiddling an evening here and there, and some make an adequate living from fiddling or related occupations. Although the only full-time teachers of fiddling in our sample are Jimmy Don Bates and Daniel Carwile, others combine fiddling with some kind of music business. Tony Ludiker teaches fiddling both in individual lessons and in well-attended fiddle camps and does a roaring business rehairing bows in rainbow colors. Pete Rolland, who has taught many hundreds of students, has a music shop with a burgeoning violin rental component. Tim Donley builds and sells wonderful violins. Full-time performers include Ricky Turpin (formerly fiddler with the country group Asleep at the Wheel, now freelancing) and Paul Shelasky, fiddler with the bluegrass group Lost Highway. Tonya Hopkins teaches privately less now than formerly, though still hiring on at fiddle camps such as those run by her sister and sister's husband, Idaho fiddlers Danita and Matthew Hartz. Joel Whittinghill has cut back on teaching considerably to make room for the more reliable income of a quality engineer, though his students still do well at important contests. Wes Westmoreland III spent a decade fiddling in Branson, Missouri, and still supplements his income as pharmacist with evening gigs. Others in our sample have fiddling as part of composite incomes, the other components of which are also traditional. These include Brian Grim (teaches fiddling half the year, shears sheep the other half, delivers mail year-round, and owns a bed-and-breakfast), Betty Vornbrock (makes elegantly upholstered instrument cases), Bobby Taylor (runs two festivals in addition to managing an archive), Lark Reynolds (a contest entrepreneur as well as health professional), and Richard Bowman (supplements his farm income with playing for square dances quite regularly). Mack Snoderly, retired from dentistry, plays as many evening gigs as he desires in the western North Carolina mountain tourist industry. In fact, every one of the adult fiddlers interviewed makes some money off of fiddling in shows or for dances now and again, and more would be full-time professionals if fiddling was more fashionable and marketable, that is, more mainstream.

"How did you get started fiddling? Who taught you?"

The younger years of today's older fiddlers featured easy and regular access to fiddling, and not too many other choices for evening fun. As Carl Hopkins said about his father E. J.'s entertainment choices: "They didn't have TVs or anything like that." Despite the availability of radios and phonographs, musical entertainment that was immediate, that offered lots of choices, and that sounded good was music they made themselves. There were then many more fiddlers and associated musicians per capita, enough to play for neighborhood dances regularly.

That Senator McLeod's fiddle mentors included both an older male relative and someone not related to him but who also lived nearby was typical for fiddlers of his generation. Kenny Sidle learned from his father, an uncle, and a neighbor who lived just over the hill ("when that fellow was sober"). Roy Crawford "came from a musical family." The only senior fiddler I interviewed who didn't trace his craft to a member of his immediate family is E. J. Hopkins, who, however, "just liked the fiddle." Interestingly, he didn't learn Texas-style fiddling when he started. That style was then still young, with wonderful but not very numerous practitioners. When, as an adult, he encountered seminal Texas fiddler Benny Thomasson just once at a contest, he experienced what can only be described as a conversion.

A similar degree of automatic exposure to fiddling would not continue into the next generation. Nevertheless, most of today's best skilled fiddlers did grow up hearing fiddling in their homes. The best practitioners still start very, very young, at least in the development of their ears. Brian Grim told me that the question was not *if* he would play a stringed instrument in a local traditional style but rather *which* instrument. Bill Rogers, a Mississippi fiddler who recently turned forty, inherited fiddling just as naturally. His grandmother told him that his "great-granddaddy was a short, red-faced Irishman, spit the eye of a man at ten feet. And what he'd do, he'd invite all those fiddlers around, and they'd start playing, and he'd sit out there . . . I don't think he played, but he listened to them play . . . Meanwhile, on the inside, starting about 4 or 5 o'clock in the afternoon, you ran in there and you set eight plates, eight forks, and eight glasses, put a pan of biscuits on the table. People ate. When they jumped up, you washed and dried real quick and set them up because there was eight more ready to eat. And that went on until about ten o'clock at night. And that was great-granddaddy's birthday—that's how he did his birthday party." Bill's grandfather soaked up fiddling at such affairs, and Bill learned from him.

Rogers also had some brief but helpful exposure to classical violin technique through a few lessons during college. Indeed, many modern fiddlers' bow arms and intonation have benefited from similar carefully rationed exposure. Tonya Hopkins learned old-time and then contest fiddling as a child in Idaho, but her technique improved in recent years owing to the influence of her younger sisters Danita and Roberta, who are both classically trained: "I could see what a difference it made with them as far as their intonation and shifting."

Figure 6. Bill Rogers, at a fiddle clinic given at the Two Rivers Bluegrass Festival in Leakesville, Mississippi, by Paul Shelasky, 2004.

The working from tapes that these fiddlers cite has become more and more important in a continuing and expanded learning process. A fiddler doesn't have to remember a tune exactly or work from any level of general impression. Tapes (and, more and more, videotapes and DVDs) allow leisurely and convenient digestion. And one can intimately study the work of fiddlers one can't spend much time with, or hasn't met, or never could have met. For instance, old-time fiddler Tim Donley wanted to learn Bill Birchfield's favorite tune, "I Saw a Man at the Close of Day." Tim learned it "first from Joe Birchfield [Bill's father], and Joe ultimately learned it from [1920s fiddlers] Grayson and Whitter. And I went back and heard the original Grayson and Whitter recording, and worked with Harold [Hausenfluck, his main teacher] on it some, and found that Joe actually played it differently from Grayson and Whitter. So now my version combines a little bit of the feel of Joe's version, but I think it's closer to the Grayson and Whitter version." Texas fiddler and renowned improviser Carl Hopkins says that he "gets together with Wes [Westmoreland so that they can] pick each other's brains." Both of them listen to tapes of legendary Texas fiddlers while driving and, when attracted by a lick, rewind the tape repeatedly. "We'll both learn it, not really knowing whether we could play it or not, but we're trying to remember it. So when we get where we're going, he'll pick his fiddle up and maybe I'll pick mine up: 'Hey, man, you remember this lick we learned coming up here?' And I'll play it to him: 'No, it didn't go that way, it went this way, and we'll get to playing around with it, and then we've probably both got it wrong." Carl says that even if he's heard a tape five hundred times: "I guarantee I'll get something new out of it."

"What kinds of music were played in your home when you were growing up? Say something about how your own musical taste developed. Could you describe your collection of recordings?"

Most of the best fiddlers grew up in homes in which the dominant music for enter-tainment was country music and fiddle music. Also, the older fiddlers (and quite a few younger ones) came from homes in which there were family string bands or bluegrass bands, so that these fiddlers grew into performing as soon as physi-cally able. But the revivalist players have less contact with traditional music in their backgrounds. Betty Vornbrock's childhood home resounded with "opera, opera, and opera," while Jim Cauthen's route to fiddling was less of a conversion and more of a return. There had been fiddling in his extended family when he grew up in Georgia, but he wasn't then old enough to take it up. Instead, his childhood home was filled with pop music. When he finally took up old-time fiddling as an adult, his urban romanticism was partly fueled by actual (if fuzzy) memories of fiddling at family reunions and such.

Just as in northern Alabama and environs, taste and personal performance style in the West have turned to Texas fiddling during the last forty years. At-home listening to fiddling has been much more varied in the West, however, much more like the eclectic taste in the families of urban revivalists. Mabel Vogt's fam-ily listened to 1940s pop music and Scandinavian music (corresponding to her mother's ancestry). Starr McMullen, who grew up in New York, inherited her par-ents' love for Broadway tunes and added enthusiasms for rock music, including the Grateful Dead, and bluegrass, before picking up fiddling while in graduate school in California. Pete Rolland and bluegrasser Paul Shelasky grew up hearing mostly classical music in the home, since their fathers were professional violinists. And young Amanda Kerr's parents have a band in Anchorage that shifts freely between old-time, Celtic, and bluegrass music. What do most of these repertoires share? It's less what they are than what they are not: they aren't Top 40, or other-wise mainstream, but rather represent choices among special tastes outside of the mainstream.

Nearly all top fiddlers have enormous collections of recordings (at least two hundred, generally more than three hundred). The Texas fiddlers supplement hand-fuls of commercial CDs with large numbers of tapes from contests and jams of their progenitors, and they often are careful who they let listen to those precious tapes.

They are apt to own swing fiddlers' recordings, while the Alabamans tend to collect some bluegrass recordings and ones by earlier Deep South fiddlers with Texas influences, such as J. T. Perkins and Bill Mitchell. But both Texans and Alabamans share a broad enthusiasm for the very best in a number of violin styles, including jazz. Daniel Carwile described his collection in detail: "One can find anything from Kevin Burke, Martin Hayes, Alasdair Fraser, Jerry Holland, Kenny Baker, J. T. Perkins, Benny Thomasson, Orville Burns, Major Franklin, Dick Barrett, Texas Shorty, Terry Morris, and Mark O'Connor to Itzhak Perlman, Isaac Stern, Pinchas Zukerman, Eugene Fodor, Midori, Stéphane Grappelli, Jean Luc Ponty, Joe Venuti, Oscar Peterson, Bill Evans, Clifford Brown, Duke Ellington, Miles Davis, Count Basie, Benny Goodman, and Charlie Parker, to name a few."

"Do you teach, and, if so, whom and how?"

Fiddle-based incomes, whether part-time or full-time, generally center on teaching. Among the fiddlers interviewed, the following have or have had from a dozen to more than thirty private students: Jimmie Don Bates, Tonya Hopkins, Tony Ludiker, Mabel Vogt, Pete Rolland, Daniel Carwile, and Joel Whittinghill. Although a few of the other master fiddlers have never had students, most have taught a bit. When fiddling is transmitted through lessons—isolated hours generally occurring once a week or less—each lesson must become a package of information that can be revisited between encounters in more than just memory. Tonya Hopkins echoed many teachers in saying, "Of course, I put it all on tape." Thus, students have a fixed example of a performance to work from, in a tradition featuring improvising. Especially in camps and in even briefer clinics, student fiddlers want to "get" as much music as possible and find that a tape recorder can store repertoire much more quickly than unaided memory. I recall a clinic given by bluegrass fiddler Paul Shelasky at the Three Rivers Bluegrass Festival in Leakesville, Mississippi, a few years ago. He offered repeatedly to play tunes for taping and to do so at slower-than-normal tempos; this was what he was accustomed to providing in such forums.

Tonya went on to say: "If they're really struggling with bowing and all that, I will tab out stuff for them too. But I don't like the tab to become a huge crutch." Not as many teachers use any form of tablature as tape performances for their students, but quite a few do add this layer of portable fixed tunes. Fiddle tablature generally includes lines across a page representing strings and numbers representing fingers, with the exact positions left to the student's knowledge of the key (for instance, whether the left-hand middle finger is in low position for an F on the D string, or high for an F#). This suffices because fiddle tunes seldom modulate (when a strain is in another key, it's the *whole* strain, so a student just attaches the fingering patterns for the new key to that complete section). Of course, some fiddlers are fiddlers rather than violinists partly because of their aversion to notation, so they certainly don't teach using notation. In general, fiddle teachers see use of any form of written notation as a necessary evil at best, a tool they strive to keep at arm's length lest it sabotage improvisation or rhythmic nuance.

These days, many young fiddlers started as violin students training in the Suzuki method, which starts off by inculcating fluid motions that are as helpful for novice fiddlers as for beginning violinists. Indeed, many fiddle teachers judiciously borrow from Suzuki. The danger is one mentioned previously, that many classical violinists who teach through the Suzuki method see fiddle tunes as short and high-quality pieces—which they are—but then imagine that playing these (and airing them in contests) can be a simple stepping-stone in learning to be a violinist. This condescending attitude annoys many in the fiddle world. But many students surprise their violin teachers by preferring to fiddle. Also, ensembles of Suzuki students have their social uses at fiddle contests. At Union Grove, a Suzuki teacher brings the only black participants into this overwhelming white subculture each year. And Suzuki-based fiddle ensembles can be popular with audiences who aren't used to listening to fiddling but can be coaxed to do so by how cute the kids are. I remember at Weiser (in 2001) such a group performed one evening. They showed team spirit and lively showmanship in a ghastly rendition of the national anthem and while accompanying cloggers. Many in the audience found the experience saccharine, but others enjoyed it and may have gained a second wind to hear better fiddling later in the evening.

Quite a few skilled fiddlers end up teaching in special summer fiddle camps lasting a week or two, which have emerged in recent decades as a major venue for transferring both technique and repertoire. How closely these camps are linked to the contest world corresponds in part to geography: fiddle camps in Texas have as their main purpose transmitting Texas style and Texas tunes in forms suited for contests, while the contest emphasis is a bit less in the West and much less in the Southeast. Tonya Hopkins often teaches in the same western camps as do her sisters, and Daniel Carwile teaches most summers in one or several camps run by Mark O'Connor.

"What are your music activities during a typical week? How many hours do you devote to each?"

Contests and conventions, although the main events that present skilled fiddlers to public view consistently across the United States, are often supplemented by other venues. Many fiddlers play for dances, nearly all occasionally play for shows featuring fiddling, many play within one or another kind of ensemble not particularly based on fiddling, and so on. Dances in rural areas were once routinely accompanied by fiddlers, precisely how long ago depending on the location. The relative strength of fiddling in the South results in large part from the persistence of the connection between fiddle and dance there. Certain small dance subcultures still—or again—involve fiddlers. In the Virginia/North Carolina/Tennessee axis, there are enough regularly scheduled square dances to keep a handful of old-time bands busy weekends.

While each contemporary traditional southern square dance has its own flavor, two basic types dominate, and those two types call on different skills from fiddlers. In either category, a single dance takes twenty to thirty minutes. This doesn't wear out the dancers, because many of the patterned figures don't involve all four couples in a square. But the musicians are playing the whole time and can get very tired. Dance evenings attended by regulars who know the figures well would be difficult for the musicians to survive if *all* of the numbers were square dances and therefore called for breakdowns for accompaniment. Luckily, dancers prefer variety. According to Brian Grim, "The dances right here around home . . . it's like four straight hours of music. Everybody knows all the moves. They keep repeating the moves over and over. It's not much that's new . . . they do a square dance, and then they want a flat-foot number, and then they want a waltz, then you play them a waltz, or a two-step." This means that the musicians get to play some tunes that are less physically taxing and must develop sub-repertoires of tunes in those genres, ones that they would seldom have a chance to air at contests, where breakdowns are king. In some other square dance evenings, most dancers are tyros and must be walked through the figures. Half the fun lies in the beginners' convivial confusion. These dances fill late evenings at the Clifftop convention and are enjoyed by both experienced dancers and beginners, just as are similar dances from Raleigh to Seattle. While there is less musical variety at this widespread type of revival square dance, the musicians can rest while figures are being explained.

Old-time fiddlers with an urban revival background may well play at city square dances. But the romantic revivalist attraction to tunes that are especially distinctive points such fiddlers' contest preferences toward "crooked" tunes, that is, ones with unusual phrase lengths, tunes that don't work well at dances. Thus, such fiddlers may play in the same *genres* at contests and dances but generally not the same *tunes*.

When fiddlers in Texas play for dances, these are often swing dances so that the better Texas fiddlers have solid experience with the dance background of this one of the several genres that they are expected to command at contests, though the actual contest tunes in contest formats don't have the dance home that breakdowns in old-time style have in the Southeast. Texas fiddlers also are equipped to play in various kinds of country ensembles. Just as Wes Westmoreland backed Mel Tillis for a decade in Branson, Missouri, Ricky Turpin had an extended stint with Asleep at the Wheel.

Most skilled fiddlers have opportunities to play at shows of one kind or another. The types vary, but one thread persists: these shows present fiddling as exciting, old, and relentlessly wholesome. Sharon Bounds has been part of halftime shows at two University of Alabama football games. The "shows" for old folks often have the fiddlers to the side, playing more-or-less continuously, while ones for kids are apt to involve explanation and in general a more formal approach. Shows that are more broadly based in terms of age groups seem to demand playing the routine hits, so every fiddler who does these must play "Orange Blossom Special" thousands of times. In general, shows have just one fiddler present and have audiences that are much less familiar with fiddling than the crowds at contests. Thus, these are not learning affairs for fiddlers but rather advertise the fiddle world in broad caricature to the general populace.

What sets contests apart within fiddlers' multitudes of public presentations of fiddling? While some jams still take place in fiddlers' homes, most transmission of fiddle tunes face-to-face but outside of a formal student/teacher relationship is at jams at contests (or at summer "fiddle camps," many of which serve as systematic extensions of the learn-while-you-jam aspect of contests). And many of the tapes of tune versions by master fiddlers that fiddlers study at their leisure are made at contests (and at subsidiary fiddle camps). And, not least in importance, hierarchies of fiddlers and of styles are worked out at contests, partly on stage and partly through informal competition through who attracts the largest crowds in campground jamming.

"Of the different sorts of fiddle music that you play today, what are your favorites (breakdowns, waltzes, tunes in unusual cross tunings, and so on)? Why? What are your favorite tunes that you play at contests and that you don't play at contests?"

The contest stage requires proficiency in more than one musical genre, regardless of a given fiddler's inclinations. In quite a few contests anywhere outside the Southeast, a player must perform a breakdown and a waltz. In the far West, where Weiser is the model, a turn on stage requires short versions of a breakdown, a waltz, and a "tune of choice" that usually turns out to be a rag (though it can be a polka, a swing tune, and so forth). And in Texas, a player who expects to survive eliminations must have a number of breakdowns ready, plus several waltzes, rags, polkas, and swing tunes. So, when a fiddler didn't answer the question as originally phrased in an interview, I'd name some pair of genres and ask which of those he or she preferred.

In Texas (and among true Texas players in the Tennessee Valley), the answer is easy. Alabama-raised Texas fiddler Daniel Carwile replied: "If I'm playing Texas style, I'm partial to breakdowns. Why? There's nothing like a hard-driving break-down. I describe it as a heat or energy that you can feel. If a breakdown doesn't have an attitude, I don't want to hear it." Kentucky's Joel Whittinghill described the experience of playing a breakdown: "I'll give you an analogy I guess: it's like passing through a prism. You go to the source of light: You see one color. . . . Some of us see the same kinds of colors, but different shades of the same color. It's kind of like that." These and other Tennessee Valley Texas fiddlers really do play breakdowns like Texans do (and Idaho fiddlers don't). But their activities and enthusiasms out-side of contest breakdowns are different, that is, they have supplementary loves that aren't in the swing music that Texans like. For Daniel, that means a well-developed and much-loved Irish repertoire and an affection for pieces in cross-tunings such as AEAC#. Joel genuinely likes waltzes and has a strong enthusiasm for bluegrass tunes, especially when he plays guitar or mandolin, both of which he commands nearly as thoroughly as he does his fiddle. Sharon Bounds made special note of playing gospel tunes for kids. In short, good Texas fiddlers outside of Texas aren't quite as focused on breakdowns as are the Texans.

The top fiddlers in Texas hesitated the least when asked what their favorite genres and tunes were. And any short delay in responding wasn't owing to de-ciding that breakdowns were far and away their favorite genre: this was a given. Before answering, however, these fiddlers thought through how to describe the richness of possibilities for variation that made performing breakdowns the genre of choice, how their taste for improvising put swing tunes in the second slot, and, sometimes, how their initial hostility to waltzes had lessened over time. I found the uniformity of response among this population remarkable. Carl Hopkins pre-fers "Breakdowns, by a long shot. . . . you can put so much more stuff in one of them, and it doesn't sound repetitious." He said he liked swing songs too, for a similar reason, that they pose an intellectual challenge, "because you have to come up with something new that you haven't ever done before. . . . usually you've got like a reserve in your head." Jimmie Don Bates went into more detail: "I don't know if it's tradition or just the fact that it's what I grew up with, but I've always been drawn to [breakdowns]. I guess it's the diversity in the tune, but you can still hear the melody line. You know, this fiddling, it's a predecessor to jazz, when you do it right, because what you're doing, you're taking a melody line and trying to embellish it and improve it but still be able to hear the melody line. That's the trick. You can go too far afield on these things. I don't know. I've just always been drawn to them, ever since I started. Waltzes? I used to hate to play a waltz. I can tolerate them now, but they're not my favorite. . . . If you have a jam session in Texas, and you're talking about Texas fiddlers, you're going to hear about 90 percent breakdowns."

The northwestern Texas-style players are more apt to like waltzes, and many are also fond of intricate hornpipes. While the difference between breakdown and hornpipe is not very clear, I believe that the relatively involved basic melodies of hornpipes accommodate systematic variation less, a limitation that matters less in the northeastern contests with their truncated versions of tunes. Also, Texas and Tennessee Valley fiddlers often spoke of "drive" as an important quality attached particularly to breakdowns, while that powerful rhythmic aspect of performance was less emphasized in the West.

All of the best fiddlers in Texas, the Tennessee Valley, and the West—in fact throughout the Texas sphere—had very large repertoires, often numbering hundreds of tunes. And in each of these three areas, the top fiddlers believe and bemoan that many other contest fiddlers, especially young ones, have tiny repertoires targeted for direct and exclusive use at contests. The casual observer at contests in the three main contest-style areas might get the impression that the top Texas fiddlers shared the alleged impoverishment of repertoire of the second rank players, since even the champions play relatively few different tunes in the contests. But that focus on stage is misleading. A few central contest tunes are heard so often in Texas contests because those tunes have the "most parts," that is, each has a developed tradition of being played with specific and plentiful opportunities for variation. The best players have enormous additional repertoires of tunes that they don't perform in contests, although fragments of or ideas suggested by those tunes echo on stage: "You can learn something from every tune," many fiddlers told me.

In the Southeast, breakdowns were favored too, and the best players had similarly large repertoires. There was, however, considerable variety in shapes of repertoires of breakdowns in active use in contests, much more so than in the Texas-style areas. All the southeastern fiddlers knew a few dozen central pieces, but many fiddlers had a specific subregional focus too or, if they personally were less attached to a specific region or specific teacher, would still have some rarer tunes that they played. For instance, Brian Grim had a tight "White Top" (refers to a local peak) focus in his repertoire (plus an eclectic selection of distinctive tunes from elsewhere), and Tim Donley, while eschewing a geographic focus within the

Upper South in tune choice, nevertheless plays many tunes or forms of tunes that have impeccable pedigrees but are rare. Both of those fiddlers represent plenty of others in the nature of their repertoire choices. There are three factors at work here. First, there are simply more fiddlers with distinctive yet clearly regional styles in the Upper South than in the younger Texas-style complex. Second, the most popular breakdowns in the Southeast are largely a different group than those at the center of Texas fiddling (though much of this separation of repertoire has come about in recent decades). Third, variation in the course of performance tends to be in the area of subtle rhythmic detail in the Southeast, which doesn't favor a small group of tunes to the degree that the elaborate melodic variation of Texas style does. Thus, the overall repertoire that one hears in contests in the Southeast can be much larger, while the repertoires in the Texas-oriented areas of the Tennessee Valley and the far West are poised between the small Texas central repertoire heard in contests and the enormous repertoires of the Southeast.

Both West Virginia and urban revivalist old-time players favored rare tunes more than was the case in the Southeast. I believe that this is a major reason that the fiddle convention where old-time fiddlers and revivalists meet most comfortably is Clifftop, in West Virginia. Betty Vornbrock, who is a West Virginia-style player (though living near Galax, Virginia), likes the West Virginia repertoires and styles because they encompass "simple tunes that are complex. And they have a feeling about them. They have that lonesome mountain kind of feeling about them. A lot of them are in a modal which we like to play in . . . not necessarily notey, but they have a lot of soul to them." Overall, this area has traditionally nurtured plenty of exotic tunes with idiosyncratic sources of aesthetic complexity and thus can be authentic in the sense of little-interrupted practice at the same time that it attracts urban types who want to like simple, authentic tunes but, deep down, would like those "simple" tunes to be relatively individual in sound and tricky in one way or another.

"What are the most valuable aspects of contests? How could contests be improved?"

Fiddlers say that they value fiddle contests for three basic reasons: because contests are important for tune transmission, because they build character, and because they provide camaraderie. Pete Rolland remarked that "contests are occasions at which fiddlers "transmit *prepared* versions of tunes." That is, they present carefully considered, polished forms on stage, often in marked contrast to the freer versions

Figure 7. Betty Vornbrock in her camp at Clifftop, West Virginia, 2001. One sign that urban enthusiasts like this contest is that there are more tents than recreational vehicles in the park.

heard in jams. Thus, contests offer models both for the process of exploring the possibilities inherent in a tune and jewel-like finished products. There's an important stage in between those two also, the "finished" versions of unfinished players, of younger fiddlers who will revise their versions many times. Tony Ludiker characterized contests as being "like recitals" for his students.

Tonya Hopkins described contests as "motivational." Starr McMullen added that the prospect of public performance "makes people practice and improves the quality of playing." Rolland emphasized that the contest as a formal system of similar events is itself a recruiting tool, that is, it "draws in youngsters via structure and incentives."

Many fiddlers find camaraderie the most important factor, fellowship both within age-defined groups and between generations, and both off and on stage. Carl Hopkins asserted that "contests are just made up of who goes." Hopkins is among the many who value campground jamming far above the formal competition, but he certainly looks happy and involved on stage too. In fact, the best testimonials to the love of the competition proper aren't in words but rather in the intent yet smiling faces, in the swaying and stomping, in the joy and wit of the music itself during the passage through a tune—in short, in the sheer sparkle of performance. Few fiddlers care to sit and discuss how much fun that is. It's obvious, and the emcee will gush enough for all. On the other hand, criticisms of contests flow freely, since fiddlers who spend endless hours perfecting versions of tunes would like contests to be suitable showcases for themselves and the music and for evaluation to be as fair as possible, and these factors are out of their control.

Criticisms of contests I have heard frequently concern the preparation for and settings of contests, their structure, how long a sample of fiddling each fiddler can present, how fiddlers adjust unhealthily to the structure of the contest, and all aspects of judging. The most eloquent criticism of the initial link between event and audience, that is, the advertising, came from Jimmie Don Bates. He found the media's routine presentation of fiddling through caricatures offensive:

> That's the media for you. You look at any contest that's advertised: instead of having a photo of the best fiddle player, or even, like, a news clip on television, you'll get the guy that has a broken leg and has about three teeth in his head and a beard down to his belly. He can't play anything—just a scratcher—but to the eye, he's an oddball, he's an attraction . . . but he's not a musician. I think that, advertising, I think it should be mandatory that if an event like that is covered, that you should have a decent fiddle player playing a decent tune so that the public can have some idea what fiddling is really all about, what it's supposed to sound like. I think a lot of people are turned off. I think [this simplistic presentation has] got a negative connotation. [As a result of it, the public] think of fiddling as basically sawing back and forth really fast on the E and the A string.

Richard Bowman mentioned one drawback at the poorly run convention in Galax—that fiddlers stand in lines waiting to play for much, much longer than they are on stage (where they can play just up to two and one half minutes of a single tune!). Quite a few fiddlers noted that short times on stage meant that many fiddlers prepared only a few tunes, focusing on winning through thorough mastery of a few minutes of material and not learning much else in terms of pieces or the spirit of fiddling. And many fiddlers favor technical polish over musicality, and often are not called on this error in judgment by the judges. These problems were summarized by Jimmie Don Bates: "Even my students, depending on where they're from and how much exposure they've already had . . . all they can think about is playing good enough to get in a fiddle contest. They want to play only the contest-worthy tunes, the more complicated tunes. And I try to stress to them that what you have to do is you have to be able to play all these old traditional tunes, whether they're complicated or simple because they're all going to teach you something. I hear that a lot in the Northwest style of fiddle playing. It's heavily influenced by Mark O'Connor and Tony Ludiker, Dick Barrett. All they've done is taken these old recordings when they've played their rounds at Weiser. Well, those Weiser rounds are four-minute rounds. You have to play three tunes. So how much stuff can you put in a song? They scratch the surface. But, there's a whole lot of them out there, they take violin in high school, and grade school, and their technical execution is immaculate. But . . . there's no fire behind what they're playing."

Most complaints about contests, however, concern judging. Not every fine fiddler wants to judge: it's grueling and largely thankless. In most cases in which the judges are buddies of the contest organizers, this isn't an attempt to rig the results; it's just that only close friends can be cajoled into being judges. But many fiddlers believe that politics rears its head too often in judging, or that judges don't succeed in being objective, or that they don't enforce the rules (for example, that fiddlers in an explicitly old-time category play in an old-time style). The fewest complaints at any major contest are, predictably, at the Texas state contest. Wes Westmoreland praised the qualifications of the judges (almost always former state champions), the lack of restriction on the length of pieces (etiquette keeps these just a few minutes long but not feeling cramped), and the size of the sample for the players that last the longest in the competition.

"How are you linked to where you grew up or to where you now live (could be attitudes, church, visiting family left behind, language, food, music, and so on)?"

The final questions I would regularly pose concern values. This first one was intended to be the most straightforward but still provoked plenty of puzzled looks. Some fiddlers said that they felt no special link to a given geographical area, but most of them replied that there was one central connection: family. A few added detail to that most important factor; for example, Sharon Bounds noted that Northport, Alabama, on the north side of the Tuscaloosa metropolitan area, was where she grew up, where she lives, where her parents still live, and where her church is.

Of course, many fiddlers live where they do because that's where the fiddling they love is performed. Jake Krack, a teenager, plans "on staying in West Virginia. That's one reason I chose chemistry [as a probable college major], because down in Charleston [West Virginia] they have all these chemical plants, and I figure somehow, with the chemistry and all the math and science that is needed for that, I could get a job in the state. It'd be a shame if [the family] moved" to West Virginia for him to fiddle, then he left to go to college. Rita Scott described another link between her home and music: "I didn't like [old-time music], you see,

Figure 8. Mark Ralph and his sons, who are learning to fiddle, at home in Huntsville, Alabama, 2003. They are standing in front of his gun case. He is an avid outdoorsman and skilled hunter.

when I was growing up. I thought it was terrible. But then after I—when I was living in Winston, and being homesick, I can remember listening to Ricky Skaggs and Tony Rice, one of their records, and remembering: that's stuff that Albert [Hash, her eventual fiddle teacher] used to do." Still other fiddlers linked outdoor activities with home and with fiddling. For instance, Mark Ralph, who now lives in Huntsville, Alabama, bought some land near his Kentucky childhood home and hunts there when he has a chance. And, while he's there, he fiddles in the evening: "You can't hunt after dark." Similarly, E. J. Hopkins said that he always carries his fiddle to deer camp.

The most eloquent and detailed description of links between home and heart came from Bill Rogers, who now lives in a historical family house, one he has restored considerably:

> Yeah, this area is very special to me. I'm really into the history of my family, and the history of South Mississippi, anything historical like that . . . After I got married and moved away from home and come for a visit, I'd say to my Dad: "I'm going to walk up to Grandma's house." He'd say: "There's nobody up there." I'd say: "I'm going to walk anyway." I'd walk up here, and make a loop around, and walk back, and a lot of times I'd come up here, and there'd be nobody here, and I found that real hard to understand. Then one day she told me: "When you were a baby, this is where you lived." [She] said: "We kept your Mom and Dad living with us. You lived in this house shortly after you were born." And I've always felt more so that this was my

house, as long as I can remember. But the things I was . . . I don't know . . . I can see my grandfather coming out with a hoe handle, coming out of the porch over here, coming out of the garden. . . . I can remember we had a lot out here. We would work with the cows, and hear them lowing, and I can remember . . . I think about the trees. And I'm going to offer you some pears: I've got fresh pears on the trees out here. I think about that. We had different people who would plant cotton and soybeans. I think about the little creek that runs down here, at the bottom of the hill. Probably I associate more than anything else, aside from the fact of my grandparents being here, is this huge pecan tree that's in my back yard. And in that book [a memoir by his grandmother], there's a story, and it's going to explain to you why that pecan tree is so big. [The tree was nourished by a WPA- and Eleanor Roosevelt-sponsored outhouse, therefore named the "Eleanor."] But the county forester said that that may be the biggest [pecan tree] in the county. Because it's huge; it's magnificent. When you drive up, you can see the tree towering over the house . . . My parents are close by, and this is just home. It just feels like home. I'm driving further to work now than I did when I lived in Columbia, but it's just [that] when I drive down that road, it's almost . . . there's a period of about eighteen years that's taken out of my life, where I wasn't living up here, but it's like I slipped right back in. My neighbors, church . . . oh, they're wonderful. I love it. . . . When I grew up, . . . most of the work that I did was fieldwork. We hoed cotton, we hauled hay, we hauled watermelons. And all those people I grew up with, they're still here. They look a little bit older, [but] they're still around and just kind to me.

"What sets fiddlers apart from other Americans, other than that they fiddle?"

Some fiddlers feel that fiddlers constitute a group with a distinctive character, and some do not. Sharon Bounds said "I've thought about this question a good bit, and I really don't think fiddlers are any different from anyone else." Tim Donley bases his opinion that fiddlers are not a distinctive population on his feeling that "everybody has a creative energy in them." Mabel Vogt went beyond adamant to annoyed. She had heard opinions on this matter often enough that they had festered: "The normal platitudes in this area are just generalizations, and are also voiced by practitioners of riding, roping, bowling, baseball. Sorry I can't [chime in]. There're all kinds of fiddlers, and we form great friendships, but I won't say they're better that other people, or that they have any special moral or family values. I meet good people everywhere I go."

More fiddlers, however, do see fiddlers and associated musicians as a population that can be characterized, one made up of unusual personalities, of nonconformists. Richard Bowman opined that fiddlers are "different natured." E. J. Hopkins said that fiddlers are "all crazy" but apt to be quite different from each other otherwise. Rita Scott felt that "most fiddle players are crazy. Probably you could put them in a class all theirselves, I guess. I won't say fiddle players, I'll just say musicians. I think it's the way they try to live their lives." Here she was referring, I think, to the many old-time fiddlers in the North Carolina/Virginia/Tennessee intersection who make a point of pursuing aspects of traditional life despite the inconvenience and considerable cost. Brian Grim was more explicit on this point, and also separated local old-time musicians from urban revivalists: "Well, most fiddle players are pretty eccentric, I guess, especially the ones that . . . get involved in trying to 'preserve' the tunes and 'preserve' the music. And most of them lead a pretty simple life, or *want* to lead a pretty simple life, I guess, the ones I know, anyway . . . You don't see many of them in high-falutin' society. But there are several I do know, some fiddle players up in Maryland and the D.C. area, they're doctors and lawyers, and stuff like that . . . the musicians in the cities: you'll find a lot of them driving Volvos, stuff like that. Out here, everybody's got a pickup truck." Jake Krack valued how fiddling brought these two groups together: "There are doctors at a festival. You come out to festivals—you're all one." Young Amanda Kerr feels that "almost all fiddlers get along really well. It's almost like there's a fiddling vibe that can bring everyone together." Other fiddlers echoed the remarks concerning fiddlers' orientation toward the past.

Several fiddlers commented on the social responsibility of fiddlers they knew (see Richard Bowman's comments in the appendix). Pete Rolland guessed that fiddlers indulge in less criminal activity on the average than the general run of Americans, and he was among quite a few that felt that fiddlers can have sizeable egos. Jim Cauthen drew a line between traditional fiddlers and modern ones on that score: "Pretty good-sized egos? At fiddlers' conventions, yes, and in the revivalist scene too, but not the older avocational fiddlers [he and his wife Joyce] met." And several fiddlers spoke about the relationship of fiddlers to their music, that is, that good fiddlers feel strongly about fiddling and try to do their part for tradition by putting something of themselves into versions of tunes. E. J. Hopkins was quite clear on that score, saying that fiddlers ought to "put something of their own" into tunes. Ricky Turpin said that a good fiddler has "got to be emotional . . . The best players eventually put theirselves in it."

Nearly every fiddler felt that most fiddlers have a good sense of humor. Many of the male Texas fiddlers linked that sense of humor with energetic joking and inebriation. According to Jimmie Don Bates: "Most fiddle players that I've been around, and I've liked, and [that] played well, most of them drink, probably to excess, and every one of them had a really good sense of humor." He also agreed with Wes Westmoreland and other Texas fiddlers that there are plenty "of practical jokes going on between fiddle players, a lot of pranks pulled." Jim Cauthen had noticed in Alabama that there were a fair number of drinkers in the older generation but fewer among the youths. Bill Rogers also referred to misbehavior in the past:

> Mr. John Stewart, who's also a fiddler, told me that's what they would refer to the dances that they used to have would be the frolics. And JerryAnn's [Bill's wife] grandfather tells an interesting story about he played for one, I think maybe his brother played, or even was just a dance one night, they were playing, and Mr. Hughes' brother, who's her grandfather, asked this lady [if] she'd dance with him. So they started dancing. And the lady's boyfriend was there. And he got mad, and he grabbed Mr. Hughes' brother by the throat, and Mr. Hughes said he took his fiddle and he bashed him over the head with it. [He] busted his fiddle, and he said, when that happened, the host blew out the lantern, and they all went home. He said they came back the next day and put the pieces of that fiddle in a shoebox.

In fact, I found that the open drinking that is taken as normal in the West is no longer part of the approved public image of fiddlers in the East, despite the fact that some of those fiddlers certainly indulge. At conventions such as that in Ashe County, North Carolina, drinking is restricted to very discrete pulls on hip-flasks during jams in back corners of the campground. In fact, my plan to interview one old-time fiddler was discouraged by several others, who called him an obnoxious public drunkard and therefore not typical of fiddling and not worth my while. In sum, I would say that drinking is taken to be part of masculine and independent high spirits among male Texas fiddlers, but not in the East.

"What values does fiddling support?"

Most fiddlers took the word "values" in this question to mean what are generally considered to be positive, wholesome values. Several of these broad values were connected directly to tradition, the most prominent among this group being qualities that come up in most discussions of fiddling: family and community. Tony Ludiker summarized this eloquently: "There's a deep sense of community among the fiddlers I know. One of the strange things I feel about my fiddle friends is that we're involved in a continuous jam session/meeting of some kind. Take the National Fiddle Contest in Weiser, for instance. From year to year we just take up our friendships as if we've never been apart. It's like a gathering where someone leaves the room for a moment, then comes back in and joins the conversation

Figure 9. Kenny Sidle, at home in Newark, Ohio, 2003. Many senior fiddlers have a wall like this one, packed with trophies.

again. Even should someone miss several years at Weiser, when they get back it's like they never left." Brian Grim asserted the primacy of family: "This friend of mine that I started teaching fiddling to, he was so impressed by seeing other people, and their kids, playing this music, and those kids were less apt to be involved in running around, doing drugs, and stuff like that, he got his whole family involved in playing music. He got every one of his kids involved playing an instrument. And they're the best-behaved kids: they're never in any trouble, or anything like that." And Mark Ralph talked about how fiddling spans the generations: "I think an interest in fiddling is responsible for developing a lot of strong friendships that otherwise probably would not occur. I know that as a kid of thirteen or fourteen years old, I had a lot of 'fiddling' friends that were fifty, sixty, or seventy years old and I think that was a very good thing . . . very common in the fiddle world, but very rare otherwise." Kenny Sidle talked about the musicians in his family, and how he had written a waltz for each grandchild.

Several fiddlers talked about fiddling as something uniquely American. Starr McMullen invoked "American cultural heritage," and Lark Reynolds said that "fiddling teaches the value in the preservation of an American art form." Jimmie Don Bates, while explicitly *not* linking fiddling to Mom and apple pie, said that fiddling helped develop "an appreciation for American music."

Rita Scott was the most thorough in linking fiddling to other aspects of older rural life, and in noting how this separated relatively traditional fiddlers from urban revivalists: "To me, if you play old-time music, you need to at least understand where it came from, and try to have some of that in your life. It's . . . I don't think you can really play it unless you try to live it." "How does one live it?" I asked. Her reply:

> Well, it's not hardly possible in this day and time, but you need to at least be aware of what people did during those times. How they got their water from the creek, raising animals, a lot of the songs are based on things they used to do: "Cluck Old Hen," you know. It's hard for me to know how somebody who lives in the city, who doesn't have a clue about that lifestyle [could play the music with understanding]. I wish I could live that way. My friend Amy—she plays the banjo—she lives that way. She raises her animals, they do all their farm work with horses, they live the way that they play . . . for the people that really understand the meaning of the music, it represents what a life should be. You know: family, friends, home.

"Do you feel that a lot of fiddlers feel that, or just some?" "Well, you need to kind of define categories of fiddlers, and there's a bunch of them. There's the young kids that live in New York that have heard it on the old Folkways records, and think it's cool, and play it, but they don't know the lifestyle, and I'm not sure they have any values. That's ugly, and I didn't mean it that way. It's hard to know what they . . ." "They're the niche-carvers." "Right." "They think that'll make them different. I guess there're some city folks that have a very strong sense of nostalgia that they can't attach to their own family . . ." "Right, and they latch onto it because . . ." "There it is! There's the old way." "Yes, there's a lot of that. I tend to stay with fiddle players that I think are genuine. We call them cornbread."

But one need not remain purely an urban revivalist forever. Betty Vornbrock discussed this as part of a more general evaluation of how she as a woman and originally an outsider had come to fit into the masculine- and insider-dominated fiddle world:

> In places where there are plenty of wonderful women fiddlers, and plenty of wonderful men fiddlers, women don't seem to rise to the top. But those are all contests, and [at] contests you have no idea why. But it repeats. No matter how enlightened the judges might be, even if they're female judges. I don't spend a lot of time dwelling on it, but there are other things, like the local contest, the Sparta, the Mount Airy, and Galax, and Fries, and those. Women win plenty of things, whether they're local or not, but the local ones come up—there's always that: local people are going to win sooner than the far-away-address people, unless there's an exceptional standout. But probably overall, if you were going to ask anybody "Who's the top five fiddle players? Who's the top five banjo players?" you're going to come up with men. . . .

Am I an outsider? Yes. Am I an outsider sort of hippie type? Yes. Am I an outsider female? Yes. So is that three strikes against me or what? But I get people, if they're overlooking those things, I get the kind of compliments that mean a lot. I get people locally, saying . . . they don't seem to be comparing me to, Tommy [Jarrell] or to Emmett Lundy, or to somebody, they just take me at face value. They either like me or they don't, but they're not telling me if they don't, you know, they're listening to the music of it, or they've been touched by something of it, and that's what means the most to me. And I get men and women both doing that, and I get probably more feedback that doesn't put me in a category of being "different."

Quite a few fiddlers found that fiddling fostered responsibility to one's self and to others and independent thinking. Sharon Bounds cited self-reliance and individualism, and Pete Rolland and Lark Reynolds discipline. Jim Cauthen found individualism coupled with nostalgia:

I really like this music that came from a time when you didn't have so much uniformity in music. To me, when I listen to modern American radio, it all sounds alike somehow. They've formularized it . . . Of course, people say that about this music too, but when I go back and listen to [old-time hillbilly] music from the '20s and '30s, I hear all sorts of different sounds and approaches to the music, and so . . . I really like having that diversity to the music. . . . I think that something's changed, because I think that people at one point [at the time that they] grew up, there was more music around . . . personally around them. It wasn't something that somebody else did, because . . . I've noticed that people can't dance anymore . . . And I really do want people to hear all this really interesting music. . . . Yes, and there's a little bit of evangelism about it [on my part], because I really do want people to hear something else than the Top 40.

Some fiddlers, especially many of the male Texas fiddlers, scoffed at fiddling matching up with wholesome values. Jimmie Don Bates said: "I don't really understand what kind of family values you could get out of a fiddler's contest. A lot of these old tunes, even the lyrics to these things are pretty vulgar. They weren't meant for families . . ." Wes Westmoreland was going the same route when he said that

really there's no redemption to it. And fiddlers can be a pretty sorry lot. And a lot of them get together—and I've been just as bad—and get [drunk], play, and have fun. No redeeming qualities to it, other than the fact that it's been carried on for generations . . . [but] There's a respect. Hey, those guys were before you. And you're learning on top of what they made up. They made the tracks that you're making already, and they made it up with no help . . . and changed it, and made it as good as they could make it. . . . If you don't pay homage to them—and I've seen people be disrespectful, and it makes me fighting mad—and if you don't pay homage to them, you're not doing the history right, you're not doing these people right . . . And there's a lot of heritage involved with it. There's a lot of respect for the older dudes that a lot of kids don't give them. Anyway, we're getting into a pet peeve area now. That bothers me—I stamp it out where I can. As far as redeeming qualities, you know it's something that's been going on for years, and you don't want it to die down.

Tonya Hopkins gathered most of these themes together:

Even different contests kind of have a different mood and feel to them. I think that some of them really do promote tradition and family values and stuff like that, but there's so many different kinds of people that fiddle that there's not one answer to that. I think everybody has a different perspective. I do know a lot of people that get their kids started in this thinking that that's what it's going to be, and some of them stick with it, and some of them don't, but the musician's way of life isn't always real traditional and conducive to family values. I mean, if you asked my parents, I think they would have real mixed emotions and feelings on that one as far as what it's done for their [four fiddling] daughters. They feel like it's been the best thing that's happened to us, and the worst thing in some ways.

"And what would they think was the best and the worst about it?"

I think that it's been the best thing for our self-esteem. We've been successful with it, and we've enjoyed it, and it's something that, my sisters and I, we meet up at various contests around the country, and compete against each other, but have fun with each other. And my parents love going, and we've made so many good friends through the music, so they know how passionate we are about it. And they know that playing music takes a certain amount of discipline and that that helped us through school, and everything else in our lives, and is something to feel good about. As far as the bad, I think that sometimes, the lifestyle of being up late and playing in clubs and being around a lot of partying and [questionable] language. . . . I think sometimes certain moral issues come into question, late at night, and stuff like that, in a lot of settings it seems with the music. When your kids are young, and you put them to bed early, then that's not usually an issue, but the older they get, then that usually becomes an issue for most parents whose children fiddle. Because there's always been certain things that have always been acceptable with musicians, and a lot of parents wouldn't agree.

CHAPTER FIVE

Styles and Meanings in Southern Fiddling

I have discussed the historical context of modern fiddling, the official face of contests as competition, the festivals that surround the competitions and enrich their meaning, the fiddlers up on stage and down in the campground . . . What's left? The tunes themselves, and paths of meaning from individual performance and individual fiddler through style and event to southern American fiddling as a whole. In this final chapter, I'll start by looking at a few tunes in a moderately technical way. Then, following that tightest focus of the book, I'll close with a last visit to a great fiddle contest, a visit during which I'll try to bring the themes of our fiddling together.

Basics of Tunes and Styles: "Leather Britches"

The essential musical material of a fiddle tune is surprisingly compact: two or occasionally more short sections, each of which is repeated several times to complete a performance. Each section or strain is eight measures long (almost always), divided into two symmetrical phrases. The two strains of a tune, one of which starts out higher than the other (I refer to them as a low and a high strain), generally share quite a few musical ideas. I label the strain usually played first in a given tune as A (it can be either the low or the high one). Thus, the usual form of a performance can be represented as AABBAABBAABB and so forth. It's amazing how rich performances can be, given how straightforward and brief these original musical thoughts and customary forms are!

I have used contrasting performances of one common tune to exemplify the broadest differences between the sound of old-time and of Texas-derived contest fiddling (see figs. 12–14). "Leather Britches" has been among the twenty or thirty most popular fiddle tunes throughout the South for at least the last eighty years, the period for which considerable documentation is available in the forms of commercial recordings (starting with the "hillbilly" recordings of the 1920s), field recordings, and lists of tune titles. It entered the fiddle world as "Lord MacDonald's Reel" in late-eighteenth-century Scotland. Its title is of a fairly common type, one which associates a melody with an individual, who might be a dedicatee (the case here) or the fiddler who wrote it or a fiddler or dancer who featured it in his performances (as in the case of another common tune that has withstood the test of time, "Durang's Hornpipe"). "Lord MacDonald's Reel" retains its original title in the British Isles, in Canada, and sometimes in New England. It has flourished continuously in print and in performance in the United States since British-derived tune collections entered the mainstream of American publications in the early nineteenth century.

We don't know when "Lord MacDonald's Reel" became "Leather Britches" in the South. The younger title falls in the largest category of American fiddle tune titles, that of miscellaneous colorful down-home expressions. "Britches" of one sort or another turn up fairly frequently in such tune titles; "Leather Britches" is an old country term that refers, evocatively but ruefully, to the wrinkled appearance and contrary texture of dried string beans. By the time of hillbilly recordings, this tune was usually known as "Leather Britches" through most of the United States outside of New England. This high correspondence between tune and title is typical for common tunes, although rarer tunes can have looser associations with several names. I should note that catchy, rustic, grin-inspiring titles seem to matter more in the Southeast than in Texas.

The late-eighteenth-century "Lord MacDonald's Reel" has intricate "sawtooth" contours in both strains (fig. 10). The Scottish notations of that era present quite a bit of detail, showing plenty of ornamentation. (The "tr" used so frequently here is an abbreviation for "trill," but, following contemporary practice, that indicated just a rapid turn: for instance, the note "A" with a tr over it would be played as a very quick A, a very quick B, then the rest of the notated length on A.) In addition, a nice variety of rhythms are made explicit (as in the first two measures of the B strain). The publisher of this collection, famous Scottish fiddler Niel Gow, also made some variation techniques clear. Most tunes in his "Complete Repository" (and dozens of similar publications) have just two strains, but the second one often has a repetition written out with at least a few passing notes changed. A very few tunes receive fancy variations like those in late Baroque violin art music, just enough to show that Scottish fiddlers could match the many virtuoso Italian violinists then working in England at their own game. But a few more tunes, perhaps 5 to 10 percent by my rough count, had third strains, sometimes clearly different

Figure 10. "Leather Britches," Three Versions.

1. "Lord Macdonald's Reel," from Niel Gow, *Complete Repository* (1792)

2. "Leather Britches," as played by Brian Grim (Virginia, 2001)

3. "Leather Britches," as played by Jimmie Don Bates (Texas, 2000)

from the first two sections but sometimes, as in "Lord MacDonald's Reel," transparently derived from one of the main two strains. Here the A strain (I called it A for consistency with the later American versions, in which the one labeled A is usually played first) also appears an octave up, and so here is labeled A↑. Every American fiddler worth his or her salt recognizes this tune, whether he or she plays it or not, making it a natural choice for illustrating the most basic differences between southeastern "old-time" playing and the family of Texas-derived contest styles.

Brian Grim's "Leather Britches" follows very local practice in lacking the A↑ strain. He told me fiddlers in surrounding areas employ it but not fiddlers in his immediate community. (Style areas are at their smallest in the Southeast, perhaps because they coalesced long before the age of the automobile, not the case for the Texas-derived styles.) His version is typical of old-time fiddling in quite a few other ways. There are lots of double stops (though fewer than average for the style here), and rhythm seems at least as important as melody. Variation is found in every performance by a good old-time fiddler, but it's incidental and rhythmic in nature: note the differences between A1 and A2 and the slightly different openings of B1, B2, and the second half of B5. Seems simple so far. But much of the emphasis in a typical high-quality old-time performance reaches past what the fiddler does. In old-time music, ensembles center on the fiddle playing not quite in unison with a banjo played clawhammer style (in which a finger beats down percussively in alternation with the thumb closing, itself producing melody notes and drones, a performance style that descends directly from blackface minstrelsy). That intimate heterophonic duet acts as a composite melody accompanied by a guitar's bass note (and, likely a double bass's note) on the beat, plus a percussive guitar chord off the beat. The essence of the performance is the flavor of the heterophony, that is, how the banjoist's idiomatic and personal form of the melody matches and departs from the fiddler's idiomatic and personal form of the melody, which notes are emphasized by each instrument—the fiddle's down bows are relatively strong, as are the notes struck by the banjoist's finger rather than thumb—and how the drones produced on each instrument (generally through adding an open string, or holding on to a note just played in the melody, as here) emphasize moments in a tune and also important notes in the key. The "sound" of the fiddle melody can't be separated from the delicate complexity of the composite sonic texture of the ensemble.

Texas fiddling, and by extension most contest performance, is more oriented toward melody, both the relatively involved original contours that begin a performance and the subsequent pervasive variation of those. The melody is always there, and always audible, but the surface is in constant and fascinating flux. The version transcribed here from the playing of Jimmie Don Bates is relatively compact. It was not played for competition (such a performance would have been half again as long) and certainly doesn't reflect the even more leisurely and luxuriant unfolding of ideas typical of jamming. Instead, he played it during a ceremony installing a friend in the Texas State Fiddling Hall of Fame. It was meant as a moment of homage; its unusual brevity allows an especially clear demonstration of the essential features of Texas fiddling. He was accompanied by two guitarists playing chunky, crisp jazz chords in the typical Texas manner, but much more of what matters in the performance is contained in the fiddler's line in contest styles than in old-time music.

In Bates's "Leather Britches," each strain presents variation in a significant and systematic way. His first A strain is more different from that part of "Lord MacDonald's Reel" than is the A strain of Grim's old-time version, and his A2 ventures a bit further away immediately. We can notice that A↑1 in Bates's performance is more conventional in historical context, that is, more like that strain in earlier versions; yet A↑2 is the most varied strain in contour and in rhythm and covers nearly the widest range. The drama of A↑2 is followed immediately by the very most conventional shape in the performance. Indeed, A3 reaches not just back to A1 for symmetry, for having a form of A near the end much like a form at the beginning, but rather reaches past A1 to the memory of the parent tune, "Lord MacDonald's Reel." Then, B↓1 provides another kind of special symmetry. While A↑ takes A *up* an octave, as in the parent tune, B in Texas versions takes B *down* an octave in its opening measures. Bates's last strain, A4, offers a compromise between his A1 and his A3, a summary of forms of the most important gesture of the tune. The resultant total form of the performance is logical and dramatic, a kind of musical narrative very different from the texture-based complexity of old-time versions, which can vary in length quite a bit without changing the general effect. Put more simply, the old-time versions show their historical affiliation with dancing by being able to vary in length on the spot, that is, having a tune's length in performance gracefully subservient to function. Texas fiddling, which coalesced after the link between fiddling and dancing had become weak, can focus on forms determined by exclusively musical needs, and is more wedded to situations where the audience is listening attentively, and especially to contests.

Style and Variety in Old-Time Fiddling in the Upper South: "Mississippi Sawyer"

Gradually, during the last half-century or so, the repertoires of the complex or old-time styles and of the complex of Texas-based contest styles have diverged, losing

Figure 11. "Mississippi Sawyer," first strain, as played by three fiddlers (in 2001)

Figure 12. "Mississippi Sawyer," as played by Betty Vornbrock (West Virginia, 2001)

most of the considerable common ground they shared in the early years of record-ing. By the 1980s and 1990s, widely traveled tunes such as "Leather Britches," while remaining well-known, were played less, while tunes especially well-suited to one style complex of the other were played increasingly more. For example, "Dusty Miller" is now much more common than "Leather Britches" in Texas fiddling, and "Mississippi Sawyer" has pushed aside journeyman tunes like "Leather Britches" in old-time performance.

The earliest appearance of "Mississippi Sawyer" that I know of was printed in 1839 in the first edition of George P. Knauff's *Virginia Reels*, a collection that in-cluded quite a few black-face minstrel tunes.[1] Minstrelsy, which had been an ingre-dient in circuses and other blue-collar entertainments for some time, would burst into massive popularity and the forefront of fashion in the early 1840s and need a swift infusion of music. Knauff was an odd duck, a music teacher and general musi-cal professional living in the backwater of Farmville, Virginia. His *Virginia Reels*, a set of four pamphlets of fiddle tunes transcribed for piano, was intended for the use of "nice girls" attending "female seminaries" to learn a few facts and more orna-mental and administrative skills to prepare them to run genteel households. This collection is one illustration of a broad general principle, that overall popularity can shape fashion in unexpected ways. Here, a body of tunes with crude original associations found a second home in refined society. Of course, such tunes also remained in oral tradition.

It's no surprise that "Mississippi Sawyer" entered the public record about when minstrelsy became the dominant American public entertainment. The typi-cal quartet of early minstrelsy is the direct ancestor of the twentieth-century old-time ensemble. In mid-nineteenth-century minstrelsy, a heterophonic (almost unison) duo of fiddle and what is now called clawhammer-style banjo was flanked by players of tambourine and of bones. These last two percussion instruments, which emphasize rhythm, have been replaced in modern old-time performance by guitar and bass, which, while providing a harmonic backdrop, retain a percussive quality and thus considerable rhythmic function.

---

1. This collection was printed by Baltimore publisher George Willig Jr. "Mississippi Sawyer," which appeared in the fourth pamphlet, was there titled "Love from the Heart," while the title "Mississippi Sawyer" was assigned to another, more obscure, tune in the first pamphlet. Several tunes in this fourth pamphlet have later lives in min-strelsy but, like "Mississippi Sawyer," don't yet bear their customary minstrel titles, although these other tunes have titles that are closer in subject than are "Mississippi Sawyer" and "Love from the Heart." The future "Boatman's Dance" is here entitled "Ohio River," while the future "Buffalo Gals" is called "Midnight Serenade" (remember that the lyrics of "Buffalo Gals" includes the phrase ". . . and dance by the light of the moon"). Only the very rare twentieth-century tune "Such a Getting Up Stairs" already has its title in this fourth part of the "Virginia Reels," "Sich a Gittin' Up Stairs" (see Goertzen and Jabbour 1987).

"Mississippi Sawyer" is especially suited for old-time fiddling as that style has evolved in recent decades. In tunes in early field recordings and commercial 78 rpm records of the 1920s and 1930s, vigor was valued above precision. Today, headlong vigor remains indispensable, but another quality has been increasingly regularly joined with that forward push. The fiddle and banjo duo has become more complex in sound, more of a feathery intimate dialogue. Judges at contests like to hear the explicit delicacy of the partnership, and to have the support from guitar and bass resonant but lucid, never overwhelming. There's no longer any need to seek volume at the expense of refinement; microphones and amplifiers let any band generate enough decibels to be heard over dancers' clacking shoes, and there's more public exposure through contests than in dances anyway. In short, the constantly increasingly complex effect of the old-time bands that wins at contests now can work well at dances too, so that approach has become dominant.

At the same time that the more involved interplay of fiddle and banjo has come more and more to the forefront of performance in the Southeast, the added rhythmic vitality contributed by small, rhythmically based variation has increased. The tunes that accommodate such variation most easily are ones written with broad contours, that is, *not* ones with sawtooth-shaped contours such as that of "Leather Britches" or ones that are intricate in any way. "Mississippi Sawyer" entered modern times as a reasonably well-known tune, then became the most ubiquitous standard owing, I believe, to the flexibility of the opening gesture, a slow descent of a fifth from high A (on the E string) to D (on the A string). There's plenty of room in the melody for personal decisions about the basic shape of the tune, and players regularly take advantage of this; compare the beginnings of the performances of Betty Vornbrock, Richard Bowman, Tim Donley, and Bobby Taylor, all well-regarded old-time fiddlers. Also, as a performance proceeds, most fiddlers add intimate rhythmically oriented variation. Many subtler instances of such variation don't lend themselves to transcription, including tiny anticipations, small shadings of volume, and so forth. But melody is treated too; see the partial transcription from the fiddling of Betty Vornbrock.

The differences between these fiddlers' versions of "Mississippi Sawyer" are partly personal decisions, partly influences of teachers or friends, and partly evidence of local or regional styles (Burman-Hall 1975 and 1984). But even though aspects of regional style may be easy to hear—for instance, West Virginia styles tend to be "notier" than Virginia styles—modern mobility has muddied the picture. For instance, Donley, who learned to fiddle in Virginia, has lived near Charlotte, North Carolina, for some years, and Betty Vornbrock, who came from the Midwest originally and who plays in West Virginia style, lives quite near Galax, Virginia, because her husband has a Christmas tree farm near there.

Modern Texas Contest Fiddling: "Dusty Miller"

"Dusty Miller" is now among the half-dozen tunes most frequently played in Texas contests. Just as "Mississippi Sawyer" seems to have appeared just when the style it now exemplifies coalesced (minstrel fiddling, now called old-time), the oldest version of "Dusty Miller" that I know of comes from the earliest years of Texas fiddling, a version from 1925 by Captain M. J. Bonner. The performance of it that I transcribed (see fig. 13) is noticeably more elaborate than our Texas example of "Leather Britches." The fiddler, Wes Westmoreland III, is about the same age as fellow multiple state champion Jimmie Don Bates. While both men are virtuosos with distinctive styles, they employ similar variation techniques. I've recorded "Dusty Miller" several times from each of them. Bates's versions of "Dusty Miller" are as long as Westmoreland's, are roughly as varied and dramatic, and, indeed, have similar ingredients. The dramatic contrast between Bates's Leather Britches" and Westmoreland's "Dusty Miller" is not evidence of different approaches to Texas fiddling, but rather issues from the different natures of the tunes.

Each feature of Bates's "Leather Britches" that I used to illustrate how Texas style differs from old-time style is taken a step or two further in "Dusty Miller." First, there are yet more distinct strains: there are three, plus an octave transposition that bears differences from its model apart from its higher setting, so arguably four strains. Each strain is set apart not just by its starting with a distinctive signature lick in that strain's initial range but by also presenting a different musical topic or effect. "Dusty Miller's" A strain is about modal complexity and ambiguity, moving constantly from major to a special take on mixolydian mode and back (it contains many G sharps, but more G naturals, many of which push upwards in pitch a bit). The B strain growls on the G string, the C strain (between A and B in initial range) involves slides as an integral element, and C↑, while clearly a transposed form of C, abandons the slides marking C in favor of crystalline clarity in what is now a sawtooth contour (this being prepared in C2: compare the first measures of C1, C2, and C↑1).

Second, the types of variation in rhythmic density seen in "Leather Britches" are explored even more dramatically and systematically here. In this "Dusty Miller," A2 starts denser than did A1 (as is typical), then B2 is thinner than had been B1, foreshadowing the contrast between A3 and A4. In fact, *every* pair of strains features a contrast in rhythmic density in the opening measures. It would be possible to continue exploring complexities in this performance for pages, but the basic point is clear enough: the relatively rich possibilities of the starting point, that is, the tricky building blocks of "Dusty Miller," are matched by intricacies in execution both on the micro level and in overall form. "Dusty Miller" exemplifies for Texas fiddling what "Mississippi Sawyer" illustrates for old-time fiddling, the concentration in modern fiddle repertoires on tunes that allow free reign for the *intensification* of the historically characteristic features of the styles in which they are customarily played.

Just as there are numerous personal takes and regional styles in old-time fiddling, there are both personal approaches and regional styles in contest fiddling (although many old-time players and other critics of contest styles say that contest fiddling "is all the same"). These regional variants have emerged recently and remain controversial. The broadest divisions are among modern Texas fiddling, contest fiddling in the West (shall we call this Weiser style?), and the Tennessee Valley approach. Several famous Texas fiddlers settled in the Northwest in the later decades of the twentieth century—notably Benny Thomasson and Dick Barrett—and Weiser style came to approximate Texas style as a result. Several factors kept the northwestern style a bit different: the heritage of influence of more straightforward older styles that came with population movement across the top of the United States, the fact that the Texas fiddlers exerting an influence in the Northwest were older and not too technically aggressive, and, perhaps especially, the regional contest format. In Weiser and its satellite contests, tune presentations are shorter by statute, on the average about half to two-thirds the length of a contest performance in Texas. Weiser performances have less time for broad plans of variation (and less variation in an average measure), and feature less aggressive rhythmic emphases and less detail in form, substituting (to my ear) smoother bowing and a more crystalline timbre, a closer-to-classical sound. Performances of breakdowns in the Tennessee Valley vary quite a bit in character—sometimes being quite close to Texas fiddlers' performances, sometimes showing the influence of bluegrass (a bit more chromaticism appearing early in a version, less tidy forms)—and genres other than breakdowns tend to be distinctive.

To summarize: in both old-time and Texas-derived contest fiddling, modest melodic raw material is dealt with in complicated ways that characterize the respective styles in order to build marvelously rich performances. Indeed, as the contest setting has increased its dominance and matured, the trend toward more complexity has been constant in all fiddle styles and may even have accelerated in recent decades. At the same time, the two broad style complexes remain healthy as such, and each fiddler's style meshes personal decisions with regional styles, which persist in old-time fiddling and have come into being in recent decades in Texas-derived contest fiddling. But what happens when contrasting styles meet in competition? Last, might varieties of approach in performance reflect somewhat different opinions about what fiddling means?

Styles and Meanings in Southern Fiddling

Figure 13. "Dusty Miller," as played by Wes Westmoreland III (Texas, 2003)

Wrapping It Up: Comparing Styles and "Performing" Nostalgia at the Tennessee Valley Old Time Fiddlers Convention

The Tennessee Valley Old Time Fiddlers Convention takes place in Athens, Alabama, the first full weekend each October. The setting is welcoming, the feel of the event comfortable; it's a strong and representative fiddle contest in every way. It's physically located between centers of old-time and Texas fiddling, so it makes geographic sense that the competition itself brings together both common structures of fiddle contests, that is, both the performance medium-oriented organization of the Southeast and the age-oriented organization of the West. The contest also includes a variety of styles and thus witnesses different takes on what American fiddling is about.

Although the city of Athens is small and unremarkable, the locale offers considerable variety. Huntsville, about twenty miles southeast of Athens, is where I took my daughter Kate to Space Camp several summers; she played astronaut using real equipment that is part of the U.S. Space and Rocket Center. And south of Athens, one can boat in the Wheeler National Wildlife Refuge on the Tennessee River. Athens got its start through proximity to that river. Expeditions of flatboats passed down this section of the river in the 1780s. The surrounding area was then claimed by the Cherokee and Chickasaw (and by the British, and soon by the state of Georgia). In 1806, squatters who had rafted from Roan County, Tennessee, created the first settlement in what is now Limestone County, Alabama. The United States Army evicted them twice—honoring a treaty with the Chickasaw—but the squatter settlements became legal in 1816, the year Alabama was officially carved from the Mississippi Territory and two years before Limestone County was surveyed. Schools opened soon after the young settlement of Athens became the county seat in 1819. The Athens Female Academy, founded in 1822, is the direct ancestor of the home of this fiddle contest, Athens State University.

Entertainment in early Athens included horse racing, cockfights, dogfights, and fisticuffs (Dunnavant 1995, 17). A theater soon flourished, balanced by the founding of churches. And fiddling must have gone on, though without entering the public record. The tale I related earlier of the immigrating Bailey and Acton families meeting and likely fiddling in this general area in 1814 is the first record of a local tradition. Joyce Cauthen's study of Alabama fiddling yields information concerning fiddling elsewhere in the state that must also reflect practice in the Athens area. In one of many citations mentioning slave fiddlers, she noted that British visitors to a slave market in Montgomery in 1853 observed some sixty blacks "all dancing to the music of two violins and a banjo" while another slave called out dance figures (1989, 7). And at the same time that slaves fiddled, imitators of them were heard even more, through the theatrical institution of blackface minstrelsy. Many troupes originated in the North and toured Alabama frequently for nearly a century, from the late 1840s through 1938. The last group Cauthen documented, Milt Tolbert's All-Star Minstrels, visited Cullman, about forty miles due south of Athens (14). Minstrelsy had changed during that century, of course. But the groups of twenty to forty performers of the late nineteenth and early twentieth centuries— variety shows concentrating on contemporary materials—often contained an old-fashioned quartet playing mid-nineteenth-century frolic songs, which borrowed many melodies from existing fiddle tunes or became fiddle tunes later (for instance, "Old Zip Coon" is now "Turkey in the Straw"). And local minstrel troupes, many of them staffed by blacks after the Civil War, kept these repertoires strong. It would be hard to overstate the importance of minstrelsy in developing the rhythmic textures of southern fiddling and in nourishing and distributing repertoires. Among the tunes Cauthen cites as having been performed by blackface minstrels in nineteenth-century Alabama (15) are some that I hear every year at the Athens fiddle contest, among them "Arkansas Traveler" and "Golden Slippers."

Much of Athens State University's earlier history remains in evidence physically and in legend. The fiddle contest takes place on the porch of Founders Hall, which was finished in 1844. A local tale has it that a jug of whiskey was left behind during the construction of the four large columns that grace the front of the building. One version holds that a slave worker secreted the jug in the growing column and was unable to retrieve it when work recommenced: halting group work and calling attention to the jug would have gotten him into trouble and lost him the whiskey anyway. Another version appeared in the 1901 obituary of master mason James Brundidge: "In that day it was usual for workmen to have whiskey on all buildings and he carried a bottle there early one morning and, setting it down in the bottom of a column went to work. [He forgot about it as the work continued.] Soon the brick work was so high that it was impossible to get the bottle out without taking down a large part of the work and the stuff was just too cheap in the good old days to do that. He just left it there and there it remains" (Dunnavant 1995, 26–27). During this period, when the school was under the aegis of the Tennessee Conference of the Methodist Church, the four columns were given enduring nicknames: Matthew, Mark, Luke, and John. There's no telling which disciple now has custody of the well-aged whiskey.

Today's Tennessee Valley Old Time Fiddlers Convention stretches from Friday evening through around midnight on Saturday of the first weekend in October. Most out-of-towners camp both nights. A few participants, including the judges, stay in hotels, but the main temporary residences remain crowds of RVs parked for free on a large lawn south of the campus or in school parking lots. It's a typical festival array of similar dwellings packed cozily, an imaginary small town of the past temporarily reified. I've tented, slept in a drafty old VW van or cramped station wagon, and occasionally welcomed the judges' cushy privilege of indoor bedding at the Comfort Inn.

The main stage is set up on Founders Hall among those columns named for the disciples. About three thousand folding chairs arc out from the stage. The festival fills a few dozen acres, that is, most of the university. The nearest rows of craft stands and eateries flank the ranks of seats. This is where the half-dozen fiddle sales stands appear, along with several tables of CDs and tapes, plus other stands sponsored by political parties, the Limestone County Historical Society, and the National Association of Retired Federal Employees. More craft stands extend on both the south and especially the north side of Founders Hall. Raffles supporting a local theater and various student organizations offer chances at donated tableware and country music CDs. Crisis Services raffles a lovely quilt: I've bought enough tickets over the years to have purchased it outright by now. All sorts of campus groups who aren't in the raffle crowd try to raise money too, generally at food stands, the profits from which are swelled by the fact that the sponsoring (and profiting) organizations staff them for free.

The craft show provides worthwhile entertainment on its own. The craftsmen include the usual arrays of garrulous retirees and of stay-at-home moms whose kids are growing up, plus other hobbyists. Over a decade of visits, I've purchased oak side tables, concrete stepping stones with stained glass insets, and a clock with numerals randomly attached above the inscription "Who Cares?" (reflecting what Falassi called the festival "time out of time"; 1978). The craft show parallels the fiddle contest in critical ways: the various crafts are, like good fiddling, possible to "perform" by regular folks. The items are small and in comparable series like fiddle tunes. And community is all-important. The craftsmen/salespersons place more emphasis on conversation than on completing sales. In fact, those sales seems incidental to the craft fair, yet at the same time indispensable, nicely parallel to the fact that the fiddlers' actual face-to-face competition is necessary somehow, yet routinely pooh-poohed by the competitors.

It's a fairly big contest, with a substantial purse. Total paid attendance has run well over twenty thousand in recent years. The audience spans generations while emphasizing older folks, like most such assemblages at fiddle contests. It really is family entertainment, both *for* families and often *by* them too. When younger fiddlers are on stage, their guitar accompanists may look like older versions of the fiddlers, or wear the alert compassion of teachers, or both. Many of both the old-time and the bluegrass bands center on siblings. And even the heat of the contest

Figure 14. Mark Ralph, competing in Athens in 2003. Daniel Carwile, the accompanist, is Mark's friend and fiddle and tenor guitar teacher and has competed against him at this contest year after year.

fiddling among the best illustrates the figurative brotherhood of fiddlers. Most of the best fiddlers are at the same time the top guitar accompanists. When Daniel Carwile competes, his accompanists are usually Mark Ralph and Cassidy Koonce; then when Mark competes . . . the reader can run the permutations. Many years, Daniel will be on stage several times as a fiddler, more times accompanying his similarly virtuosic friends, and many more than that accompanying the kids that make up his large fiddle studio. Yes, he and the other top fiddlers are quite serious as contestants, but friendship and a general love of the fiddle world trump the hunger for victory easily and always.

I enjoy this event's hybrid nature, that is, that it leads off with the many performance-medium-based categories of the Southeast, then proceeds to the various contest fiddle categories defined by age as in the West (see table 3). It thus resembles the Mississippi State Contest and the Tuscaloosa affair already described: this is the regional shape for contests. Other general aspects of the contest fit national norms. The ticket fees support a good cause, here Athens State University's scholarship fund, which has benefited to the tune of well over a half-million dollars over the years (the Athens State University Foundation and the Athens-Limestone Chamber of Commerce cosponsor the contest). It's a major event for the university, which closes all offices early the Friday it starts, and assigns plenty of administrators, faculty, and students to help; the cochair of the fiddle contest as of this writing, Rick Mould, is dean of University Relations.

Table 3. Tennessee Valley Old Time Fiddlers Convention, 2004

Events on Friday Evening	Number of Competitors	1st Prize Money	2nd Prize Money	3rd Prize Money	4th Prize Money	5th Prize Money
Harmonica (finals)	13 (1 woman)	$100	$75	$50	$25	$10
Mandolin (finals)	10	$100	$75	$50	$25	$10
Bluegrass Banjo (finals)	15	$100	$75	$50	$25	$10
Dobro (finals)	8	$100	$75	$50	$25	$10
Dulcimer (finals)	12	$100	$75	$50	$25	$10
Old Time Singing (finals)	33 (15 women)	$100	$75	$50	$25	$10
Events, Saturday						
Beginning Fiddle, 10 and younger, finals	20 (14 girls)	$100	$75	$50	$25	$10
Beginning Fiddle, 11–15	20 (6 girls)	$300	$200	$100	$75	$50
Guitar, Finger Picked, finals	11	$100	$75	$50	$25	$10
Senior Fiddle	9	$500	$350	$250	$100	$75
Old Time Banjo, finals	16 (1 woman)	$100	$75	$50	$25	$10
Classic Old-Time Fiddle	15 (1 girl)	$500	$350	$250	$100	$75
Guitar, Flat Picking, finals	15	$100	$75	$50	$25	$10
Bluegrass Band	7 (3 w/women)	$750	$500	$300	$200	$100
Junior Fiddle	22 (7 w/women)	$500	$350	$250	$100	$75
Old Time Band	10 (6 w/women)	$750	$500	$300	$200	$100
Buck Dancing, 15 and younger	?	$100	$75	$50	$25	$10
Buck Dancing, aged 16+	?	$100	$75	$50	$25	$10
Fiddle King (final event)	2	$1,000				

Note: Saturday Evening Finals (five competitors/groups) in these categories: Beginning Fiddler (i.e. aged 16 and under), Senior Fiddler, Classic Old-Time Fiddler, Bluegrass Band, Junior Fiddler, Old-Time Band, Buckdancing (aged 15 or under), Buckdancing (aged 16 and over; preliminary rounds in both dance categories had been on another stage during the afternoon. The final play-off for Fiddle King between the Senior and Junior champions, then the drawing for the door prize of $300 ($200 had been awarded on Friday night).

When the competition starts on Friday night, the harmonica players lead off. In the 2004 contest, one woman plays, and three boys, but the rest of the baker's dozen of competitors are amazingly skilled older men wearing bandoliers of harmonicas. We hear arrangements of fiddle tunes and of old songs, plus a handful of hymns and "The Star-Spangled Banner," which has become a harmonica standard. Next up are the mandolinists, most playing fiddle tunes, all male. The next groups, the bluegrass banjoists and dobro players, all are guys too, as are the dulcimer players this year. Why not more women? Perhaps it's partly the heritage of men tinkering with physical devices. And perhaps it's partly a holdover of the nineteenth-century custom of women being relegated to supporting instruments, which in the fiddle world would be the guitar and bass. Those are indeed the plucked strings that most women instrumentalists command here. They strum *accompanying* guitar only (though never for the flashiest fiddlers). Women have made the most inroads as soloists in fiddling itself, although championships rarely come their way (save occasionally in the Northwest, where a more classical sound is acceptable). There seems to be something ineffable not yet shared between genders, something about guys with salty personalities learning from each other that adds the final aggressive polish to a breakdown.

Friday evening closes with the longest and least skilled bracket, old-time singing, a gender-balanced category. We hear old tearjerkers ("Rosewood Casket," "When the Wagon was New"), broadside ballads old and older ("Amelia Earhart," "Galveston Flood"), even the occasional Child ballad ("Gypsy Davie" and "House Carpenter" in 2004), a few moderately funny songs ("The Preacher and the Bear," for the fourth year running), and plenty of religious standards. This roster doesn't stretch to the recent record of forty-four contestants in this category, but my suggestion that we judges get combat pay isn't considered very funny.

The audience assembles slowly Saturday. At 8:30 A.M., when the youngest fiddlers start, their parents and friends and a few diehards dot the sea of chairs. Just three of the ten-years-old-and-under batch play fluently, but we encourage them all (silently rejoicing that a Huntsville Suzuki violin teacher who brought a horde of cute absolute beginners the previous year was discouraged from returning: we know what Gatling gun spray of bullets we have dodged). This is the first year that the beginners have been separated into two brackets, with just the older group having finals in the evening. (We do continue to tinker with the shape of the contest. We started an hour earlier on Friday than in previous years, and a half-hour earlier Saturday. Is the contest growing too large, and are the perils of gigantism looming?) The beginners aged eleven to fifteen include quite a few exciting young players. Over half of both groups of youngsters are girls, as are most of the prize winners, matching a gender shift nationwide. We have yet to see a woman become the "Fiddle King"; perhaps it's just a matter of time, perhaps not.

The day continues with the bracket for finger-picking guitar (no girls here!). Then, with the senior fiddlers, those over sixty, we enter a critical bracket; the winner here could conceivably be the Fiddle King at the end of the day. Fiddlers representing very different styles populate this bracket, and judging would be very difficult in an apples-versus-oranges way if these fiddlers weren't at such a variety of levels in terms of technique. Some play like the old men they are, illustrating both the lower overall standards of technique of earlier times and also the deterioration of ear and hand that time delivers. Other seniors remain quite skilled, but the actual contest is for second place unless Roy Crawford isn't entered (that is, after two years of winning a given category, he must sit out a year, a common fiddle contest mechanism). His clean and long bow, excellent intonation, and distinctive approach (poised in a happy spot between bluegrass and contest styles) mean that he wins, and goes on to face the junior champion in the final fiddle-off. But all of the senior fiddlers do their best, offer us personalized slices of fiddling's past, and are rewarded with appreciation both for their music and for their endurance in the world of fiddling, an appreciation symmetrical with that accorded the children who played earlier in the day.

Then comes old-time banjo, the frailing and clawhammer styles described in connection with the contest in Galax. Many of *these* banjoists are revivalists, who are apt to play with more headlong enthusiasm than with the refinement characteristic of these styles as practiced to the east. And there's little sense of the central repertoire of the East. I love it anyway. Next comes "Classic Old Time Fiddle," a bracket created here to protect the less flashy older dance-oriented styles. It's another very uneven bracket, here populated to a great extent by urban revivalists, but great fun. Flat-pick guitar follows (young guys, most of them fluent), then bluegrass bands, here usually a smallish bracket with a handful of established bands and another handful of pick-up groups, who can be fun to hear, trying to click as ensembles. It's late in the afternoon, and diehards who have listened to the whole series of short tunes are worn out. But excitement is on the way.

Nothing beats the sheer star power and lively playing of the junior fiddle bracket. The word "junior" is more than a little deceptive. It's everyone between fifteen and sixty; it's most of the best fiddlers at their best. Neither the joy exhibited nor the prevailing atmosphere of informal friendliness wane during this category of competition, but layers of intent control and proud satisfaction in mastery of the instrument are added: this is the most obviously competitive part of the contest. Each fiddler is allowed a breakdown and a waltz (as in many contests), and the repertoire narrows, especially for the breakdowns. In his interview, Texas champion Wes Westmoreland spoke of the "strong" breakdowns possessing lots of "drive" (rhythmic power), and of having "a lot of separate parts," that is, consisting of more stable strains than the two that most fiddle tunes start with. Indeed, the tunes Wes cited as "strong" and as therefore generally scoring well (that is, "Dusty Miller," "Tom and Jerry," "Grey Eagle," and "Sally Johnson") were among the handful of breakdowns heard over and over again at this contest far away from Texas. Focusing on these few tunes allowed direct comparison of versions and of performances and, paradoxically, gave a greater impression of variety than the larger number of less "strong" tunes heard in some of the other contest brackets. Also, the waltzes that are played the most are strong in another way, in containing plentiful double-stops, or especially graceful and varied ornamentation, or unusual vivid harmonic changes. All in all, the best players play the tunes that are hardest to explore fully, and the level of excitement ratchets up considerably.

The other most-loved categories are the two band brackets. Neither group represents as vital a tradition as in the Tennessee/Virginia/North Carolina orbit, but they're inherently exciting and a stimulating switch from the solo brackets. The old-time bands tend to be urban revivalists from Birmingham (for example, Jim and Joyce Cauthen's group, called Flying Jenny) or from as far away as Greensboro, North Carolina. An occasional rural string band can turn up, however, as have Bill Birchfield and the Roan Mountain Hilltoppers now and again—their voyage to Athens quite a bit easier than that of the emigrants from the same county who founded the first Euro-American settlement in this part of Alabama two centuries before.

Few established bluegrass bands come to Athens, leaving some demand for pickup bands. Indeed, that's the main attraction of this particular bluegrass band bracket: skilled players get together and take a group flier on trying to be an instant yet exciting and competent ensemble. Individual breaks within a song can be solid, and some of the interaction between musicians will be extra suspenseful because we know how fragile the new partnerships are, how hard the players must be having to concentrate, and what serendipitous good moments can suddenly emerge from performances—which are also replete with just-getting-acquainted blunders. At any rate, the ensembles give us in the audience a change of pace before we return in the evening for the finals in various categories. The top five scorers in most categories face off, with scores wiped clean. The audience fills all of the chairs for the first time, intent listening becomes the rule, and talk of what is going on on stage interweaves seamlessly with the ongoing convivial chatter: "That's what he played last year." "She's developed a goiter?" "His waltzes are improving." "Pass the catsup." "Where's that fiddler, you know, Daniel [Carwile]?"

All the usual tensions plus a few burgeoning ones pass in review on the stage on Founders Hall, making extra clear that this fiddle contest is a dynamic event within an intensely lively subculture. The overriding judging issue is always "authenticity and taste," a phrase placed in quotes here because these words constitute one of the five categories on these judges' score cards (the others being "rhythm and timing," "creativity," "expression," and "execution," lined up in that order on the forms, but with "authenticity and taste" in the center of the list and right at the heart of the process). At this contest, authenticity is both a general concern and a specific issue within the fiddling divisions. On the list of judging criteria that the competitors are given (within each category-specific, longer rules sheet), creativity and authenticity are seen as balancing, and the explanations seem addressed especially to fiddlers. Under "Creativity," the rules read: "The judges will listen for minor variations and improvisations. However, the creativity should not be excessive so as to change or destroy the basic melody line of the tune which will result in a loss of points." Then, under "Authentic Performance Style," the rules read: "Excessive and indiscriminate changes in a tune which makes the performance unclear or unrecognizeable, or the addition of inappropriate modern 'licks' will result in a loss of points." Every year, the judges assess small transgressions of the letter or spirit of the regulations. There is usually at least one fiddler whose style aligns his performance with the junior or senior bracket (that is, with Texas-derived contest fiddling) who seeks refuge instead in the classic old-time fiddle bracket, which he correctly perceives as being populated by less technically adept performers. Of course, since there always can be a grey area between contest and classic styles, the judges' individual inner debates about what qualifies as "classic old-time" style can lead to surprising finishes for fiddlers in that bracket. The fiddler *I* (as a relatively strict judge) assigned to last place among the five finalists in 2004 ended up winning (I thought he was too bluegrassy for the bracket), and my top choice ended up in fourth place.

But, as always, the greatest drama and most telling illustration of ongoing tensions in the fiddle world came up when the "junior" fiddlers competed. The group was uncharacteristically thin at the top this year. Brandon Apple of Arkansas was the winner of the bracket and overall "Fiddle King" the last two years and therefore could not compete (he *was* at the contest, jamming all over the grounds). Five-time winner Daniel Carwile, Mark Ralph, and Sharon Bounds, the most skilled "junior" fiddlers who had lived for decades in Alabama, were absent for one reason or another. The only reasonably local fiddler entered who had a solid record placing in this bracket was Kentuckian Joel Whittinghill, an exciting player who takes lots of chances not all of which pan out. And Californians Tristan and Tashina Clarridge had come to town (as a detour from a trip to Nashville for a gig). Tristan was fresh from once again winning the "national" contest in Weiser, Idaho, and Tashina would go on to win in 2005. They are wonderful clean players in what I've been calling the Weiser branch of Texas fiddle style. Joel, Tristan, and Tashina all

Figure 15. Tristan Clarridge, of California, competing in 2006 at the Tennessee Valley Old Time Fiddlers Convention in Athens, Alabama. He and his sister Tashina were headed for a gig in Nashville, but friends convinced them to compete.

played solidly in the preliminary round and made the finals. Tashina left for the Nashville gig, leaving Joel and Tristan facing off. Joel played very well, and none of the chances he took—and they were many, as always—resulted in audible errors. But Tristan's fiddling was technically immaculate and quite musical. As a partisan of local style and fan of the underdog, I held my breath as places were announced. To my pleasant surprise, Joel won (and would go on to be Fiddle King this year).

The next morning, I chatted about this over biscuits and gravy at the Comfort Inn breakfast buffet with judges who'd been in on this decision and with other folks in earshot at the buffet, musicians who turned out to have been competitors in other brackets. I asked several shifts of diners how they would describe the differences in style between Joel and Tristan. Answers centered on a factor that makes Tennessee Valley contest fiddling distinctive, the character of the waltz. Tristan's waltzes, said one local musician after another, had been too slow, lacking in "danceability." This detail of authentic performance is not mentioned in the contest rules and is not as characteristic of waltzes in the Texas fiddling on which Tennessee Valley fiddlers model their breakdowns. It is, however, a quality that fiddlers in *this* region require in waltzes, a genre which they like more than do Texas fiddlers anyway. Idaho-style waltz performance has neither the common Texas flavor ("I have to play a waltz now, but I'll 'attack' it because I wish I was playing a breakdown") nor the singable and danceable character of the Tennessee Valley approach to waltzes. The western way is to parlay waltzes with incredibly complex double stops into wistful character pieces. In any case, Joel's victory, based on his regional approach to playing waltzes, illustrated the slowly growing acknowledgment of new regional contest styles.

What other changes in fiddling might this contest illustrate? The most important symptom of change is that it's getting a little bigger, like many contests, but not all of them. A long-term pattern continues to play out, one in which fiddle contests in small towns tend to grow, with a new one added now and then, while those in large cities tend to shrink and eventually disappear. This general trend is clearly evident in our sample of contests. One of the endangered contests, the Mississippi State Contest, held as part of the state fair each fall, was in peril of losing its funding a few years ago. It will probably remain in jeopardy, although a flurry of letters at one moment of crisis temporarily stabilized the funding. It costs very little to put on, but the fair commission has little reason to remain supportive. While the state fair resonates with the same old-time values as the tiny fiddle contest within it, the contest seems less tied demographically to the event within which it nests than are the other features of the fair. The contestants and most audience members, that is, those there specifically for the contest, buy a ticket to the fair and pay for parking, walk through the fair environment on their way to and from the contest, and overpay for a greasy lunch, but that's the end of the interaction. This small crowd simply goes home after the contest. Yes, a few other folks attending the fair wander by the contest tent, walk in, and perhaps are intrigued enough to find out more about fiddling. But that helps the fiddle subculture, not the state fair, as these potential new members of the fiddle world sit at the contest instead of spending more money at the fair. Some such contests have ceased to exist in recent years, and many others are, like this one, becoming increasingly marginal.

And the Tuscaloosa contest that I described at the beginning of chapter 1, the one held each February in a shopping mall, did lose its prize money in 2005 and became an open-mike jam for a year. The merchants of the mall who had put up the prize money for some twenty-five years doubted that the contest still earned its keep, that is, stimulated sales enough to balance the money and time invested in it. This came as no surprise; this is the last local survivor of a brand of contest once far more common in the area, that is, those held in shopping malls. Prize money was restored in 2007, but the mall has since changed hands, and the event remains in jeopardy as of this writing. Bill Lowery, the head judge at Athens, once made a business of operating such contests. In the 1980s, he had three going annually in Chattanooga, Tennessee, alone. Charlie Butler, who ran the Tuscaloosa contest for most of its life, took his cue from Bill. To start one of these contests, an organizer need only acquire a list of fiddlers to contact who live within a day's drive and convince the mall board that hosting a contest would bring in lots of shoppers. The former task is easy, but the latter increasingly hard, as fiddling's appeal to a general audience has become more and more questionable. As at the Mississippi State contest, it seemed that the musicians and their fans were increasingly separate from the physical (and mercantile) environment, again indicating that the participants had moved from being an interest group still bearing a viable link to mainstream culture to being a discrete subculture. But the vulnerability of such big-city contests is more than balanced by the creation of new contests such as the one in Moulton, Alabama, mentioned in connection with craft types in chapter 3, plus the modest but steady growth of most contests held in small towns.

The largest contests really have little or no room to grow. At Galax, unpleasantness associated with festival gigantism discourages the less dedicated from returning. And Weiser both benefits and suffers from the marvelous efficiency that its size mandates. Five minutes per fiddler, including a minute in transit and introduction, then four minutes in which to fit three tunes . . . wow. The machine spits out those who don't cooperate: a few years ago, a tremendous fiddler in the Grand Champions category, one who might well have won the contest, insisted on taking a few minutes on stage to better tune the instruments. The judges, irritated by this delay, penalized him for this transgression, and he was out of the running. This ruthless enforcement of the tight scheduling is applied evenhandedly but hurts contest fiddlers from the Northwest less than those from elsewhere. The local fiddlers play in styles channeled over the decades by this contest format to emphasize quick exposure of virtuosic technique rather than the systematic variation of the Texas-style fiddling of the South and particularly of Texas itself, and thus helps keep the "national" contest truly a regional one, which in turn helps minimize the pressure to grow.

Medium-sized contests are finding schedules just a little more strained each year. The Texas state contest, the most serious one in the United States in recent times in terms of featuring head-to-head confrontation of champions, seems to be losing its much-needed comic relief bracket (the Texas Jackpot, with its blowing of air horns or clanging of cowbells when contestants don't know an obscure tune the title of which was drawn from a hat). With increased numbers of contestants in the "real" competition, that bracket is now described in event publicity as taking place "if time permits," and time has not permitted the last few years. In Athens, the effects of incrementally increasing numbers are more modest so far. We found that we needed to start an hour earlier each day starting in 2004 and tried a bit harder to be efficient.

Nostalgia is the key to the enduring popularity of this event and the key to the health of the fiddle contest subculture. Indeed, nostalgia is critical to all sorts of related cultural processes worldwide. Ray Cashman, in a recent article titled

"Critical Nostalgia and Material Culture in Northern Ireland" (2006), found that "by preserving and displaying local material culture of the past, Catholics and Protestants alike grant seemingly obsolete objects new life as symbols necessary for inspiring critical thought that may lead to positive social change" (137). Plows and such that were being thrown away in the 1950s through 1980s when more modern tools became available are now honored as physical traces of a time when adherents of the two religions managed to get along in order to farm successfully. While modern agriculture requires less cooperation, thinking fondly about a time when these two groups of citizens were interdependent economically and really did manage to coexist reasonably happily is a great idea. No one would claim that nostalgia always works to unify, but examples like this one abound. The rosy tinting of memory characteristic of contemporary nostalgia, when meant to inspire action, is at least *intended* to color that action positively.

The southern American fiddle world presents a much more complicated case than that explored by Cashman, since music in general and fiddle tunes in particular are much more open to interpretation than (to continue comparison with Cashman's study of Northern Ireland) farm implements. And the fiddle world varies significantly because of its enormous geographic, musical, and, I would argue, ideological scope. First, it's worth pondering the long and enduring significance of music for nostalgia. Even in much earlier times, back when the term "nostalgia" described what was considered a pernicious medical condition, men required by their professions to live away from home (notably soldiers and sailors) found that it was music that most vividly reminded them of home, and thus led to serious depression. In 1710, Swiss author Theodor Zwinger wrote about Swiss mercenaries serving in France and Belgium being deeply saddened when they heard country tunes from home (the *ranz de vaches*, a herding tune, all modern examples of which I've heard sound cheerful to me!; Starobinski 1966, 90). In a more complete roster of psychological culprits, Boym reported that "Swiss scientists found that rustic mothers' soups, thick village milk and the folk melodies of Alpine Valleys were particularly conducive to triggering a [paralyzing] nostalgic reaction in Swiss soldiers . . . similarly, Scots, particularly Highlanders, were known to succumb to incapacitating nostalgia when hearing the sound of the bagpipes, so much so, in fact, that their military superiors had to prohibit them from playing, singing, or whistling native tunes in a suggestive manner" (2001, 4). And the negative possibilities of savoring nostalgia—that is, the potential for musing on the past to the point of paralysis, for substituting rosy reminiscence for current energy—still arouse notice, as in this recent remark from then British prime minister Tony Blair: "Countries wrapped in nostalgia cannot build a strong future" (Behlmer 2000, 1).

The American fiddle world, however, follows a path more similar to the Northern Irish healthy symbolic use of material culture to fuel optimistic thought and to push away from sectarianism toward a contemporary community informed by nostalgic assertions of past social harmony. The complexities of meaning in the fiddle world have some relationship to the variety of styles, which, in turn, result from a symbiosis between musical history and somewhat contrasting current cultural needs in various regions. All of this is wonderfully on display at the Athens contest. Yes, all of the fiddling looks back to the averred virtues of historic small-town life, of community and family, and of individual creativity balancing harmoniously with local group values. But the details help fiddlers with somewhat different characters and from parts of the country with their own flavors all enjoy what they're doing. In the Southeast, the more traditional fiddlers draw especially strongly on community and continuity when they play the hits of old-time fiddling, while the numerous urban revivalists stress the quaint end of tradition by drawing on the some old-time repertoire but turning more toward tunes that are striking in terms of mode, or titles above average in quaintness, or with irregular numbers of measures. In Texas, the larger fiddle world's G-rated family values yield somewhat to aggressive masculinity, with old tunes renewed through individual craftsmanship and presented with attacks that cut and pleasantly bruise the ear. In the northwest, Texas style is toned down, mixing with classical timbre and with relatively fixed forms in a social setting that is somewhat less blue-collar, that reflects an average higher level of formal (and formal musical) education. Something is lost, and something gained. When I shed my claim to academic objectivity and admit that I prefer Texas fiddlers from Texas, I have to follow that admission by noting that I grew up in Texas, so that the attitudes and the way those are linked with musical style are bound to resonate with me.

Of course, the Athens contest has both broad divisions of old-time style as well as various subdivisions within an all-too-brief classic old-time fiddle bracket and has both Texas-style contest fiddlers like Daniel Carwile and Sharon Bounds as well as southeastern type contest fiddlers like Joel Whittinghill and Roy Crawford every year, and those closest in style to Texas fiddlers usually win. It was a surprise in 2004 to see bluegrass-influenced Joel facing off with northwestern Tristan and Tashina Clarridge, with no top fiddlers in central Texas style represented. That Joel's local-style waltz made the difference was a moment very important for preserving the regional substyles that reflect different regional histories and preferences. At the Athens contest, on Friday night, quite a few of the songs we hear are old waltz songs, ones that really were danced to by many members of the audience and quite a few of the older fiddlers.

But these differences in style, so valuable in drawing in strong constituencies in each part of the South, are modest when compared with how much the regions of southern American fiddling share. As the Athens contest draws to a close on Saturday night each year, I reflect on its inner consistencies, on the congruence between competition, living arrangements, crafts and foods sold, humor, and overall feel of the event. These factors all exemplify ways that members of the fiddle world would like to remember they have been and would like to believe they can be. At this and all fiddle contests, they keep traditional what they can, choose to believe that even more than could be traditional is, and quietly modernize when doing so is convenient and doesn't undercut the general ambience. It's surely not surprising to see some needs of the present easily overcoming intended and claimed fidelity to the past. What's impressive to me is that everything at a fiddle contest explores diplomacy between past and present; it's all memory as repaired by nostalgia, and all in the service of a specific cultural goal, of maintaining a comforting—and invigorating—picture of small-town life in a rosy past, back when people got along, tried hard to do their best, and loved a wholesome frolic but, above all, cared for family and community.

Appendix
Four Fiddlers Speak

The four interviews transcribed here were with especially articulate fiddlers from different parts of the South. Each fiddler received a transcript of his or her interview and edited for content; then I edited for space.

Richard Bowman

I met old-time fiddler Richard Bowman in August 2001 at the enormous contest in Galax, Virginia, and interviewed him at the family campsite. Richard, Barbara, and their daughter Marsha made their temporary home in a venerable smallish camper. Under a complex of tarps rested chairs placed in an arc for conversation and jamming, a homemade bass fiddle, and a small table with a few fiddles for sale as well as multiple copies of three tapes made by their band, the Slate Mountain Ramblers. The Ramblers do well in the competition at Galax and at the complex of smaller "conventions" in the area and would take third in the old-time band bracket this year, for the fourth time during the last ten years. Richard also places high nearly every year in the old-time fiddle category, Marsha has begun placing in the clawhammer banjo bracket, and Barbara, the band's bass player, places regularly in buckdancing.

C: Where were you born?
R: I was born in Patrick County, Virginia. . . . I was the baby out of eight kids. I'm the only one that really plays music out where other people can hear it. I had a brother that played guitar a little bit but just at home; he never did go out and play. My mother played the autoharp. My dad played the autoharp and the clawhammer banjo. . . .

The first thing I could remember about a old-time fiddle was I heard Tommy Jarrell, who lived in Mount Airy, North Carolina, playing on WPAQ radio station. It was like his seventieth birthday, and they had him there for his seventieth birthday party, to play music. He played a lot of them old tunes, and I thought: "Well, man, that really does sound good." I said "I believe I could learn to play that, if I had a fiddle. . . . I put myself where all of the fiddlers was, once I got started . . . and there was a lot of them. There was a lot of different tunes, and a lot of different styles, even in the county that I lived in. . . . Taylor Kimball and Stella, his wife, played; they played a lot of C tunes and G tunes. The reason they did that was because they had autoharps in the band. Them old autoharps only had the major chords on them [that is, one could play just a few chords on them]. Ivan Weddle lived in Floyd County, which is the next county from Patrick County. He played on the Parkway out there at Mabry Mill. He played in D and A, for some odd reason. Each little county, and each little section of a county, they did that. And they even played different tunes. . . .

I lived about twelve miles [from Tommy Jarrell's house], and I could go over a night during the week, and I picked up a lot of stuff from him. I also picked up stuff from all the other fiddlers too. Ernest East, Benton Flippen, Kyle Creed, all of those fiddlers was around in this area, and they were all playing in bands, and played conventions like this. They all played, and I was there. I was standing in the back, listening. And then, after I got to where I could play, I got to getting a little closer and a little closer, and then I got to playing some with them. I played with all of them but Fred Cockerham; I never did get to meet Fred in person. But I learned some of his tunes off of the recordings that they made of him later. I never did get to play none with Kyle, but I was around Kyle some. But I did play with all of those other fiddlers some. And it was fun, too, to learn all that stuff. And the last years, I guess, of course all of those fiddlers have since passed on, you know. Most of them was in their eighties when they did die. Benton is still living. And he's here [at Galax]. He just had a birthday: he's eighty-two. He's still fiddling, and still fiddling good, as usual.

C: Had your parents been in Patrick County for a good while?
R: All their lives. That's where they were born.

C: What professions did they have?
R: My mother just stayed at home and farmed with my dad—a tobacco farmer mostly. He had a few cattle but mostly tobacco. And Mom—you know, she was just always there. With eight kids, it wasn't like she didn't have anything to do.

C: And while you were growing up, what kind of music was in the house?
R: You know, it really was none, until I started.

C: Did you have a phonograph?
R: Just radio, mostly. Had a few old records, but it wasn't the old-time records; it wasn't many of anything . . . what we listened to on the radio.

C: What kinds of music did you like while you were growing up? What runs parallel to the fiddling for you, just for your own enjoyment?
R: Most any kind of string music is what I like. I like some of the older bluegrass; some of the newer stuff don't catch my ear. Not that I don't like it, it just don't catch my ear like some of the other stuff does . . . mostly the old-time stuff. But you'd have to understand why I'm like that. We've always played for square dances and for dancers, and that's what I like to do. If there's somebody up there dancing, it just tickles me.

C: What's your profession today?
R: I help a fellow on the farm, and we play music on the weekends. Still farming . . .

C: So, if you had a typical week, if there is such a thing, what musical activities would take up how many hours?
R: [We play] on the weekends mostly: maybe Friday night. Mostly Saturdays and Sundays and an occasional fiddlers' convention that lasts a week like this. It's mostly this Saturday night and Saturday evening stuff, dances mostly.

C: Do you practice alone? Just with the band?
R: We only play when we go somewhere to play.

C: So that adds up still to a good amount.
R: You know, you're talking, for your dances, it's normally three and a half, sometimes four hours, normally three, three and a half hours. You maybe take one break in between. You're constantly sitting there playing tunes, just one tune behind another.

C: What things other than music link you to where you grew up? Some people say it's food, or furniture, or family. . . . what are the sorts of things that tie you . . .

R: It's just the people that lives in the area that we live in. It's just . . . everybody plays. Some people in most all the families plays, or their grandpa played, or their uncle, or something . . . and, if you go to the family reunions or something or other you're always around that music because there's music at all of them things. If it's not your own family reunion, you go to somebody else's just to help them play.

C: The whole idea of family gets bigger.
R: Yeah, yeah. It don't have to be your family to be a family reunion, that's for sure!

C: What in your view are the strengths and the weaknesses of contests like this?
R: Well . . . I don't know how to answer that: we just like to play. We just like to get together. Here last night [at the Bowman campsite] when we were playing there was part of five bands here playing. That shows you that don't nobody get too mad or upset when somebody wins and somebody don't.

C: A lot of times I talk to people—they don't like the contest part but they like the rest.
R: Well, it's just a little aggravating to go up and stand in the lines. You get to talk a whole lot when you get up there, and you get to jam. Everybody jams right up to the back of the stage. A lot of talking going on, you know, 'cause everybody's just standing there, just a-moving kind of slowly.

C: Uh, this is kind of a hard one: if you think about the fiddlers and the other musicians that you know, what apart from playing music sets them apart from everybody else in America, what qualities?
R: Musicians are different-natured people. Somebody that likes to fish ain't going to be down in here. You've got to play music or like the music. You want to be around it.

C: But are there, like, habits of consumption, or habits of character, or all old-time musicians are tall . . . not something silly like that, but . . .
R: No . . . Look at that feller right there: kinda hefty. A good bluegrass fiddler. Teaches music, got a little music shop . . .

C: Do you have students?
R: Only the local people right around . . . in the little community where I live. . . . I don't charge nobody for doing this, but there's a couple or so, or three, that will come by one evening a week only for one hour. I only do it for one hour because when they're kids, their attention span is short. . . . If they're just trying to learn or

something . . . if you go longer than one hour with it, it gets to be like a chore for them. It don't need to be like that. It needs to be fun, and if you always leave them wanting to come back, they will come back. But if you go at it too long at a time, they don't want to come back the next week. It seems like, what little experience I've had with trying to show people how . . . I have never until just the last few years tried to show nobody because I was still learning, I was trying to go myself and learn. Now that I've gotten a little older and I'm not gone as much during the week, when we get in from work, I've got a little more time to help, and I only do that in the wintertime, in the winter months . . . in the summer months there's just too much stuff to do during the week. If you've got somewhere you've got to go for a dance on Saturday night, you've got to do all your work so that you can take off Saturday. Sometimes we have to drive two hours to get to where we need to be to play. If we go to the Carter Fold out at Hilton's, Virginia, it's a three-hour drive one way, and we usually try to leave and go back and get supper, you're talking, you're tied up all day Saturday, and plus Saturday night. It's just part of it, you know: you've got to get to where it's at.

C: Yeah, I've done a lot of that too. Yeah, you travel, and you've got to get set up and make sure things are going to go right. Kind of like Chinese cooking, get it all ready . . .
R: It usually works out fine, because all of these places that has these dances has been having them for a pretty good while. We don't play every Saturday night at the same place because we would even get tired of that. We always switch it around, and there is a few bands that helps us, of course. There's more bands than us. Sometimes we'll play once a month at the same place. Normally it ain't quite that much, because there's a lot of places around having dances in this area, because it's just a part of the way people is around here. I don't know how it is in other places. . . . Around here, within two hundred miles' radius, there is a lot of dances, so we've got a lot of places . . .

C: What's "a lot?" Twenty, forty?
R: Twenty. Twenty places. And everybody likes to dance. . . . Sometimes they do square dances, sometimes they do set dances, sometimes they just do a lot of flat footing, and we play a lot of slow tunes, because a lot of these people in some of the places we play are older people. They can't stand to dance every dance fast, so we play a lot of slower tunes, and they're old tunes that we play. I've not learned too many up-to-date tunes, because, like I say, all of those people that I picked all of these tunes up from was, when I was a-learning them from them, they was probably seventy years old. And those tunes probably goes back to their teenage years, when they was learning them.

C: Do you still listen a fair amount . . . do you have CDs and tapes and so forth?
R: Got a houseful.

C: I bet you do. And do you concentrate on old-timey? Or do you have some other stuff?
R: You know, recently, within the last year, I have been getting some CDs . . . you know, County has got out a lot of stuff. And I've been getting some, and listening to some of the stuff that they've got and put on CDs. It goes back to the twenties, from the twenties on up, as long as them old string bands was going. Here lately, I've been listening and getting a few, and learning a few more tunes. Since all of the people that I was a-picking those tunes up from are done gone, you know, I'm still learning . . . from some of the people that was not from this area. It was Tennessee fiddlers, and West Virginia fiddlers, string bands, and just . . . different places. Actually, just last week, I picked a tune up off of a CD.

C: That's good . . . you don't want to declare closure, say, "That's it. That's enough."
    Maybe the hardest question, but an interesting one for me, is: what values do you think playing this music supports in people's lives?
R: Well, when I'm hemmed up to answer a question like that, I don't know.
    [A helicopter flies by, and we discuss it for a moment.]
    All of the people that I've knowed that's in the music, as far as the values of the people is concerned . . . everybody was OK people. And they was well-thought-of people in the community that they lived in, because they did things when they needed to do things, other than just play music and have a good time. They did things for the support of the community, like the local fire departments and rescue squads, which all of the places around here has. And people that needs help with hospital bills, that has cancer problems—that's a big problem—they give benefits. We play for things like that. The people comes out, and they support all of that. They would, probably, anyway, but we go there and entertain those people while they're eating their spaghetti supper. . . . all of those people are nice people. You know, everybody that I've ever met that played music I reckon I liked. I guess I'd like everybody else that doesn't play music if I was where they's at to meet them.

Bobby Taylor

West Virginia's master fiddler Bobby Taylor no longer competes but is very busy at contests and festivals as a clinician, judge, and administrator: he runs the Vandalia Gathering and the Clifftop Festival (known officially as the Appalachian

Figure 16. Bobby Taylor playing at Clifftop (which he runs) early one morning in 2001. Though he plays in a West Virginia style, he was judging at Galax, Virginia, the next week.

String Band Festival, but everyone just says "Clifftop"). When I interviewed Bobby's protégé Jake Krack at Clifftop in early August of 2001, Jake pointed out that I ought to try to interview Bobby. To do that, I had to brave the beehive that was the administration and information tent. A half-dozen people scurried around there registering contestants; explaining schedules, regulations, and local opportunities to be housed, fed, and entertained; and selling festival memorabilia hand over fist.

I made an appointment to see Bobby at 9:00 A.M. the third morning of the festival, that is, August 4. He showed up on time but visibly the worse for wear. After working all day each day to make sure the festival runs smoothly, he jams well into the night and early morning throughout the week of the festival. We sat just a few feet behind the administration tent. From there, we could see the stage and sound equipment (still covered with dew-dampened tarps) and a colorful vista of RVs and tents, an instant village flanking gravel roads in this forest setting. That there were as many tents as RVs is one sign that Clifftop welcomes as many urban revivalists as players who inherited the music in their families and home locales; no other contest that I have attended solicits a volunteer yoga instructor.

C: How'd you get started fiddling?
B: I got started fiddling at the age of thirteen. I had visited with my father, mother, and brother. My father's name is Lincoln Taylor. As a matter of fact, we're working on possible getting him here today. He's ninety, and he still fiddles.

He decided at the age of thirteen that the fiddle that his dad in 1944 had given to him on his deathbed was his most prized possession. The thing is, he didn't trust two young boys around a fiddle until they'd become a certain age. I was thirteen; my brother was ten. I remember getting to carry the fiddle about a mile across the hill to the car, because you couldn't get to Grandma's house by car. You had to walk about a mile and a half. This was Roane County, Walton, West Virginia. But I got to carry the fiddle across the hill. Naturally, curiosity to any young boy: what on earth does this thing do? A fiddle is such a strange instrument: it seems to get the curiosity of kids. I've almost noticed how kids wonder: how does that thing work? Well, Daddy showed me a little bit of "Soldier's Joy." He noticed something really unique about my playing. Because, you see, I'm a fourth-generation fiddler. My brother picked it up and had good intonation, but he didn't really shuffle the bow. I was the opposite in one way: I could note fairly good too, but Dad noticed that I could already shuffle the bow, without ever *learning* to do it. And so I played "Soldier's Joy" that day for him. And he showed me the notes in it. But boys being boys, two weeks, a month later, he said: "Have you practiced any on the fiddle?" I said: "Well, I don't think I'm interested right now," and Dad said the only words that a father can say to a young son—kids always have that rebellious side—"Well, you probably couldn't learn *nohow*." I thought: "I'll show him." That's exactly what he had in mind. So that's how I got started.

C: Apparently, your folks have been right in that same area for a good while.
B: Roane County, and then I was born in Kanawha County, in Charleston, West Virginia. I grew up in Dunbar. I didn't move from Dunbar until about 1996. I now live in St. Albans.

C: And what were your parents' and grandparents' professions?
B: My father was a machinist for Gravely Tractors. My grandfather, great-grandfather, great-great-grandfather, they were all farming people. They raised huge gardens. They canned their food. They worked hard. They raised cattle and sold cattle for money and . . . My grandmother on my father's side did not have electricity. On my mother's side; they had gas but not electricity, so they had the old gas lights, with the little mantles and things . . . I remember going over there. But Dad's parents, John Clinton Taylor, and Arrie Ann Walls Taylor [he spells all parts of this name]—sometimes that gets wrong[ly] transcribed. Then my great-grandfather was Elijah Jefferson Taylor, . . . Paxton Taylor. And then John Oscar was the fifth generation back. And we don't have any knowledge that he played. We really think that Elijah Jefferson played, a little, because how could you have a house full of four boys who were all super fiddlers and not have tried it yourself?

It's just something . . . all men go hunting, all men went fishing: men did what men did. We figure that I'm [a] fourth [generation fiddler] because he had to have played.

C: What's your profession today?
B: I am a librarian. I'm the library manager for the West Virginia Archives and History Library, that is the West Virginia State Archives. We house the historical material for West Virginia, and we have all of the county court records pertaining to genealogy, so we have a lot of people doing genealogy in our library and those interested in . . . the state's history. We get a lot of academic people using our facility as well as genealogists.

C: Is there a kind of a connection between your being a fiddler and your profession?
B: . . . There kind of is. . . . I've always loved history; I've always loved old things. I was raised with the values of a firm foundation in the past. Today I collect antiques. I'm happy with furniture and stuff from the seventeen and eighteen hundreds—early eighteen hundreds, that is. I love the history that goes with the furniture, I love antiques, and basically, I really enjoy the stories of the old fiddlers. And there are countless stories. I could probably write volumes of books on my affiliations with fiddlers and all that. I really figure that history, where I'm at in the library, the fact that we do preservation and conservation, we try to preserve the music, we try to present it, and we have a tape collection, we have the Vandalia Gathering . . . this is a part of culture and history. The Archives and History is under that umbrella. So you see, I've always said that the music and the history and the arts and the crafts in the way common people lived before television and radio. . . . I do live in the past, and I love the past. I don't like the looks of the future. I don't like the coldness of humanity as it's veering toward the answering machine mentality and the stressed-out people and people who don't do what they say they're going to do. I come from a line who do what you say you're going to do. If I'm supposed to be here at nine o'clock to meet with you, I'm here at nine o'clock to meet with you. But the point is: old time values [are what] I like. But I've rambled on and on around your question.

C: No, no, those [answers] were going directions I would have tried to take you, in a way—the next question was: what are the sorts of things that tie you to where you grew up?—and you've given me a lot of the answers. Do you also seek out old food—that doesn't sound quite right! Do you prefer to eat historical foods?

B: I love that, and I tell you what, even though I grew up with the old traditional dishes, and stuff from the old farm people, there's nothing better than a tomato that a farmer that knows what they're doing has raised. It's much sweeter than anyone else's. My father's garden was phenomenal. His tomatoes were popular. And to this day—now that he's not able to get out in the garden too much, I raise the garden—and a few of the comments that he's made from the garden are . . . He can't see well, but he kind of puts his hand over his eyebrow and he says: "They look like they grew up in the woods." Now I take it that that is not good. And then they're not sweet. So my father's secrets are still with him. I'm not successful at raising the garden. But yes, to answer your question about old foods, I do like the standard foods, although I have acquired a taste for some of the modern dishes [of] a great chef. Mother *hated* great chefs. She would not eat anything that they would fix. She said it didn't taste like food. Now I'm not that far back. But I do appreciate the good old corn on the cob from the garden, the green beans freshly strung, tomatoes, the squash, the zucchini, and fry the zucchini up, just simple little recipes.

C: What kind of music did you hear while you were growing up?
B: OK: My father, when he found out that I had some talent, he wanted to expose me to what he considered the greatest fiddlers. And he did pick some very high challenges for me. Sam Jarvis was the first recording that I got to hear because Daddy said that he was the greatest fiddler that ever lived. Sam Jarvis's name was Reese B. Jarvis. He was a contest fiddler, and he won numerous contests. His style was extremely fluid, smooth; every note was the size of a golf ball and as true as it could be. His tone was incredible. If you hear a smooth roll to my fiddling, that is the Sam Jarvis influence, because I love his playing. Another fiddler that I like who tops my list—there's two of them—Clark Kessinger, world-renowned fiddler, lived three miles from me. Daddy took me at the age of sixteen to see Clark Kessinger. We got his recording. Now, I didn't learn to play the fiddle the way people learn it today. I learned strictly through the monkey-see-monkey-do oral tradition. I would go watch Clark Kessinger play, and then I had his record, [on which he plays] at breakneck speed. And I had to learn that way. I never realized what the old banjo picker Herschel Thornton, who started me to play in a band situation, and Bill Miller, two of my dear friends . . . Herschel is deceased now, but Bill Miller is now about 88 years old, and I still try to play with him occasionally. But, where I was trying to go with this is: those people and influences . . .

Herschel Thornton wanted to play at Red House. He calls me Saturday morning and he says: "I would really like to play 'Red Bird' tonight. Do you

think you could learn it?" I said: "I don't know." He knew full well that that
is one of the hardest tunes there is in old-time music. So I said I could learn it.
That night we played it on stage, and it shocked him to death. Me at the age of
about sixteen, about Jake's age [Jake Krack, an excellent young West Virginia
fiddler], and I played "Red Bird" that night that I had learned from a record.
And normally you have a few days to seal a tune in, you know, but I played it
that night. They told me that it was a very hard thing to do, so I didn't know
no better, so I played it. But in any case, I did get to go see Clark Kessinger, and
Clark Kessinger was a very kind gentleman to me. He was a very, very big mentor in my life. His many styles of bowing was just absolutely staggering. And he
learned from Ed Haley. El Haley had a numerous amount of bow shuffles and
styles and noting patterns that were very technical. Clark found Ed Haley, and I
asked him who his favorite fiddlers was; he would name two: Ed Haley and Eck
Robertson. So I started learning Clark's music then, and then I got introduced
at about the same time to another major mentor, was Mike Humphreys. Clark
Kessinger could bow a tune with more spirit and technique than you could
imagine. If you've heard his recordings you know exactly what I'm talking about.
Mike Humphreys was a little different. He had a lot of fire in his playing too.
But what he had was a roll similar to that of Sam Jarvis that I mentioned earlier.
He had a roll to his fiddling, and Mike Humphreys could play with such pas-
sion. He could get everything out of a note. He could roll a chord as another
note. And I once made a statement about Mike Humphreys. I said that he
played a tune with the ultimate of soul and beauty, leaving nothing else to
be done. When Mike Humphreys played a tune, there was no need for
anybody else to play it. It was just so perfect. Every ingredient was tastefully
exhibited.

C: Did you hear other kinds of music while you were growing up?
B: I was very self-centered in fiddle. When the Beatles come out, I had no interest in them. When rock and roll . . . and all my friends was playing rock and roll,
I had no interest. Not that I didn't like their music, you understand me. The volume
level is what got me. My ear . . . if somebody shouts at me, to this day I jump . . .
So to answer the question, rock and roll hurts my ears when it's played at the volume [at which] it's designed to be played.

C: Me too.
B: I cannot stand loud music. And to this day, I do love a Beatles song when I've
got control of the knob. I love "Let it Be," I love some of the tunes like Crosby,
Stills, and Nash does, but at [my chosen] volume.

C: So what do you have in your collection of recordings besides fiddle music?
B: The fiddle is just about it . . . So my focus is pretty much what it was.

C: If you have a typical week, during that typical week, what are your different musical activities, occupying how much time?
B: My father, as I said, is ninety years old. He lives with me. My father still plays the fiddle. Andrew [a friend present at Clifftop] comes over and plays with him. My house pretty much is an open door to musicians in my area. It's nothing uncommon for me to, on the spur of the moment, to have musicians come in and play for the evening. If I'm not doing music, you will catch me at the flea markets and antique shops. I am a—I am also known as "the tone hog." I love collecting good instruments and good bows, and I love rich, thick, smooth tone. And right now I'm not having a good couple of days. I've got two great bows in my case. One, the bow screw that tightens the tension on the hair is stripped out. The other bow, due to humidity or whatever—I just had it haired, and the hair is all falling out. I have done cut off twenty-five hair on it, and there's more sagging down now. So I'm almost beyond playing. I'm almost bowless now. So I'm hoping to catch one of the fiddle repair people very shortly.

C: Do you have a lot of students?
B: I could have. I choose not to teach, because I work forty hours a week as library manager, [and] I constantly either entertain or play with my friends. I then run two major competitions: Vandalia is the other one that I coordinate the competitions for, and I coordinate the competitions for this one. And then I judge at Galax occasionally. It basically gives me no time. With my father being ninety, that takes its share too, you understand. So right now, I feel like I am the busiest person I know.

C: But is Jake [Krack] your student in a way?
B: Jake is not necessarily a student. And I'll get on that tangent. To pay back what was lovingly given to me, I do agree [to], and have never turned down . . . a fiddle workshop at Augusta or Allegheny Echoes. When they ask me, I do these. That gives people a week with me to learn what they want from me. I don't turn workshops down. But I don't give private lessons. Jake's situation is something much more than a workshop or giving lessons. It is an apprenticeship through Augusta Heritage Center. I was never able to find anybody that could do the licks that I got from Clark and Mike and Ed Haley and all that. I stood alone in doing the triple bow jumps and all this stuff. No one else could do them. I honestly thought when Jake asked me—I didn't even do apprenticeships [back when he

first] asked me, and I always said to my friends: "There is two young fiddlers, if they were to ask me for an apprenticeship, I would not be able to turn them down." And my luck held until Augusta two years ago, and Jake asked me. I said: "Oh shucks, you're one of the only people that stood a chance of that." It has been the most rewarding facet of my life. Since I have taken care of elderly parents and don't have children of my own, and no one to pass my music on to, I could not be prouder of Jake. So Jake is far more than a lesson. He is the one that will carry on what I do after I'm gone. He's sixteen, and I'm forty-eight. It's time that I passed something on, and not just do a workshop where I teach someone a couple of my tunes, but they don't learn my style; they [just] learn the tunes. In this case . . . and I guess you've got[ten] to hear Jake fiddle?

C: I've interviewed Jake.

B: So Jake, as I say, is far beyond lessons. I look at him like myself when I would go to Clark Kessinger, and he showed me how to do his famous triple bow after his stroke. He sat in a chair, and I held the fiddle over here to the side up there, and noted it while he showed me the bow what he was doing. So, you see, I had no one to pass that on to until Jake. So it's not—and I'll tell you about lessons—I wish I had the talent to give lessons, and the time, and what I mean by time, as you can tell, I don't have the time. But it's a talented person that gives lessons. Jake watches every move I make. He's on the same mental telepathy that I'm on. He can actually almost spit it directly back at me, which is like he is a part—his mind is on that same wavelength, which is almost spooky. And I sit there as cold chills go up my back, thinking: "How on earth can he do that?" But Jake would be the first to tell you: "Bobby is not good at breaking a tune down." I—it's very hard for me to take a measure out of context, and tell you which notes. The reason for that, I feel, is that I am a melting-pot fiddler. I don't play anything the same way twice very often. It's just one of those things that . . . people who are learning needs to hear it the same way, so they can get it. For me to do a workshop . . . I do it, and give it my all, and think that I'm not giving enough, even though I've got wonderful reviews from students. I still work myself to death trying to think: how did I show them? And then they tell me—someone in the class with classical training will say: "You didn't do it that way last time; you did it this way." That's why it's a very major challenge for me to teach. It's a major challenge . . . something that I would have to dedicate a lot of focus. Because I have no focus. I'm like the wind that blows. I have no focus. I do what I'm inspired to do that particular minute. So, what it would force me to do is to focus and line it out. Now I've had people tab out my music, and they've tabbed it out, and I'm thinking: "[I] wonder if I can play it the way they tabbed it?"

C: If you think about the people that fiddle who you know, what sets them apart from the major run of Americans, apart from the fact that they fiddle?

B: It is a very small community of friends and musicians. Right now, if there would happen to be a major catastrophe right here, right now, old-time music would be almost wiped out, in a big portion of it, because most of them are here; a lot of them are here. So, there are very few, but they do hold, in the historical and artistic societies, they hold that special nurturing part that makes the music live on. And what sets them apart is their values, their focus, the past. They look for a way of life that is a little less stressful, even though we're not finding it these days. It takes you back to something that is homespun, that is timeless, that's historical. And it's not that other people are not historical or anything like that; I think that what sets them apart is they have picked their one obscure little nook that they really cherish, and it's like any other thing: you will find little niches of needlepoint people, even people that do bobbin lace—which is very hard to do—people that will do quilting. Little niches of people get together and cherish their own talents, what they're talented to do. But I think what sets fiddlers apart is: the hustle and the bustle of the big city of Chicago, the hustle and the bustle of New York, even though their day jobs is there, they like to come to West Virginia, where they can get back to an area that is still in the focus of what they love and really want to see go on. And that's why this festival I feel is so nice and so homespun that people feel comfortable bringing their children here. Now, after twelve years, we see the children playing. We see the children taking a part in it.

And I tell you what: to answer your question probably best, there was a young guy who was thinking about being a guitar player but wasn't sure. His father wasn't sure he could keep him interested. And I was sitting there at the table and remember giving my words of wisdom, which I still think were wonderful, even though they weren't thought out, it just come out. I said: "Well, you're young. If you decide that you want to do this, now is the time to make that decision, because you can learn faster when you're young." And I said: "I will tell you this: the music is secondary to the wonderful people who play it. And if it hadn't have been for the wonderful people in the old-time music community, when I went through the hard times in my life, watching my mother slip away for ten years, if it wasn't for those people, I don't know where I'd be today. It will add an element of quality to your life. It will give you a venue to visit with friends, an outlet for your problems. It will also . . . you won't be sitting alone on the weekend; you will have friends that care about you. If this is of value to you, do it now." And the young gentleman has done it, and that's good. So that is my story to the young people that has the talent and the interest, where if you don't have the talent, or don't think you have the talent and the interest, you're [still] part of it. You don't have to play. You can be a connoisseur of history, anybody can. And I tell you what: one of the most valuable people that I know, and I tell her this, and I don't care [if I] tell you, Emily Rogers is a dear friend of mine. Everywhere I have played, she is there in the front row. I told her that she was one of the most valuable people in the music world. I said: "If there's not somebody there to enjoy it, and to truly love it, and totally be a pleasant face in the crowd, it's not worth doing." . . . Last year, I had the most wonderful experience. As I was standing on the stage, the wonderful bands were playing. I looked out over all of these trees with the blue sky, and the setting just being absolutely tranquil. I thought: it doesn't get any better than this. I have my family here, which are my musician friends, people who I would do anything I could for, because they have given me so much.

Lark Reynolds

Lark Reynolds is among the first women to win prizes regularly at fiddle contests in the Kentucky-Alabama axis (the first to place at the Kentucky State Championship) and also a contest entrepreneur who has thought a great deal about how those events ought to be put together and administered. I met her at the annual contest in Athens, Alabama, in October of 2000, when we both were judging. At the judges' meeting before the contest started, her voice was prominent, never pushy and always laced with humor, but carrying easy authority. She was friendly, obviously very knowledgeable about fiddling, and naturally extremely busy throughout this day-and-a-half contest. We had difficulty getting together then and later, so she let me send her a short interview by e-mail. Rather than inserting her answers between the questions, as others completing the interview by e-mail had done, she printed the interview, then responded to most of the questions in the following essay.

> I was born July 15, 1970 in Louisville, Kentucky and have lived here my entire
> life. My parents are both from Kentucky as well, but grew up in two small towns.
> My father is from Green County and my mother is from Hart County, both in
> Central Kentucky. I have worked for the past 15 years at the Medical School for the
> University of Louisville. I am the Director of Health Surveillance Programs. We do
> medical/health surveillance for the chemical industry workers and the individu-
> als who live around the chemical plants in the city. We monitor the health, air, and
> water of the areas around these plants to insure that no one has health concerns that

might be related to chemical exposures. My mother is a receptionist for the Medical school, although she stayed home with my older brother and I until we were both out of high school before rejoining the work force. My father, oddly enough, is medically disabled from one of the chemical plants that I do surveillance on now. He has numerous medical problems resulting from exposure to high levels of vinyl chloride in the early 1970's.

I was first introduced to fiddling through my maternal grandfather. My mother's side of the family all plays and my initial exposure to fiddling and bluegrass came from spending most of my childhood on my grandparents' farm and in the general store they owned and ran in Hart County. My grandfather was the local square-dance fiddler and the two-story general store he ran was the site of the county's entertainment on most nights. I remember liking the music that they played, but it wasn't until I attended the Kentucky State Fiddle Championships with my grandfather when I was about 11 years old that it grabbed my attention and pulled me in. I remember standing on the hillside, late at night, during the finals, and hearing Jimmy Mattingly play that I was completely awestruck. I left that night, determined I was going to learn to play like that. My parents managed to get in touch with Jesse Haycraft, the man that had taught Jimmy and several other boys in the area (all of whom have become very well respected contest fiddlers) and convinced him to give me lessons. He had more of a classical approach, but the position work and intonation training I received from him laid an excellent foundation for my fiddling as well. I remember my first lesson. He told my father that I would never learn to play. He said it just loud enough for me to hear in the other room and become determined to prove him wrong. He laughed several years later when I was the first female to ever place in the Kentucky State Championship that he knew it would have that effect on me! Jimmy moved to Louisville after I had been playing for a couple of years, and I began taking lessons from him. I couldn't wait to get home from school in the afternoons so I could learn new tunes from him. He is still one of the most creative and inspirational fiddlers I have been around. I am not sure I could describe his teaching methods, or what made it so successful. Since I was his only student, I am not sure he had a specific plan himself. He placed the most emphasis on playing straight and clean. He gave incredible attention to each note individually and stressed the importance of that to me. He had spent a great deal of time around fiddlers like Dick Barrett, J. T. Perkins, and Pete McMahan and drew from them when he taught me.

My mother sang in a band when she was growing up in the 1950's and played saxophone and guitar. There was a mix of very traditional country artists, fiddling, gospel, and bluegrass in our home. I can remember my mother singing constantly to me as a child. I can't think of a time when music of some sort was not part of our day. We would listen to groups like the Rambo's, Marty Robbins, Connie Smith,

Flatt and Scruggs, etc. I still enjoy and listen to a variety of music and my collection reflects that. I got extremely interested in Texas fiddling in the mid 1980s when I met Terry Morris at a contest in Nashville. I had heard some of the Texas players at the Grand Masters contests that were held in Nashville, but it was Terry's playing that really got me interested in it. Although I am not a Texas style player, it is by far my favorite to listen to. I also got hooked on bluegrass music about the same time and began learning to play with bands. I worked with a bluegrass band during college as part of an outdoor drama. The musical score for the play was bluegrass and old time music.

I am linked to the area where I grew up in several ways. Kentucky is the home of bluegrass and is in the Bible belt of the South. I grew up greatly surrounded by both of these. My parents are both fairly conservative. Both grew up in church. Both grew up in small towns where you helped your neighbor and respected them too. They instilled those values in me at an early age. I think those ideals are partially responsible for the way I have always tried to approach competitive fiddling and contests for sure.

I listen to music constantly in my car, in my office, even in my sleep. In fact, my parents claim I used to play fiddle tunes with my hands in my sleep! I play daily some [days] more than others, but very consistently. I find that it calms me when I have had a stressful day, and brightens my mood if the day hasn't been particularly good. In the last four or five years I have gotten heavily involved in producing fiddle contests, so a good portion of each day is devoted to finding sponsors, judges, entertainers, and competitors for those as well. I started the contest "business" with a lifelong fiddling friend of mine, Jonita Aadland. We had grown up at contests together and wanted to do our part to ensure that they continued. We had noticed that just in the years that we had been attending them, several contests had ceased to exist. We feared a time when there would not be any contests for us, our nieces and nephews, or our children to attend. It seemed that the stark competitiveness at the contests in the recent years had taken a lot of the fun away and resulted in contests shutting down because of low numbers of contestants. We decided if we could add back some of the "fun" elements as well as picking good judges from various areas of the country, and good prize money, we might be able to generate new interest in the contests. It seems to have worked. We held the Red River Fiddle Fest in Shreveport, Louisiana, the Grand Lake Fiddle Fest in Grove, Oklahoma, the Spur of the Moment Fiddle Fest in Mesquite, Nevada and now the Starved Rock Fiddle Fest in Ottawa, Illinois and the Mt. View Fiddle Fest in Mt. View, Arkansas [the last two of these have fallen by the wayside].

My favorite tunes are Texas-style breakdowns to listen to, although, I am personally a much better waltz player than breakdowns. I think the drive of the Texas breakdowns is what I enjoy listening to the most. As far as why I am a better waltz player, I would have to attribute that to Jimmy and Mr. Haycraft's emphasis on clean playing and intonation.

I guess the difference in tunes that I would play in contests as opposed to shows or dances is probably in the arrangements. I tend to work out contest tunes and play them pretty much the same each time as opposed to more improvisation if I am playing for a show or dance. I think there is more emphasis on playing "for the judges" and the way that you put sections of tunes together when you are playing in a contest as opposed to playing more for the "entertainment" at a dance or show.

As I mentioned, I became concerned over the image of contests over the past five or six years, and even more concerned about the number of contests that now have ceased to exist. I think the emphasis on competitiveness at them and the idea that winning a contest solely determined if you were considered a "good" player (and losing them determining that you were not a good player) caused many players to shy away from them and even resent them. In reality, they can be an excellent learning source, and for many the only chance to play with and be around other musicians. I learned as much from listening, jamming, and watching at contests as I was learning to play as I did during structured lessons. This was the theme that Jonita and I decided to build our contests around. We filled them with lots of built in time for jamming and even rewarded the "Beginning/Junior" category contestants for jamming and participating with good sportsmanship. At each contest, we gave away a fiddle to the Junior contestant that best portrayed the spirit of fiddling. This was not necessarily the winner of the division, or the best player, but the one who tried the hardest more or less. A committee made up of other musicians as well as some spectators chose the winner. Also we added categories like our "Gambler Division" where all the contestants chose names of tunes from a hat. If you knew the tune, you played a short version of it (enough to convince the judges), if you didn't know it you were out! It was more of a game, where the winner was determined more by luck of the draw than by ability, enabling a beginner to beat the World Champion if they were lucky! It was a great ice breaker to the usual set up of contests and allowed the audience to hear a great selection of tunes that fiddlers probably would not have played in the contest, very old time tunes, show tunes, jazz tunes, obscure waltzes, cross tunings, and forgotten breakdowns for example. We also added a "Let's Get Wild Division" which was a category judged by the audience more or less. How many times have we all been to a contest where the audience didn't agree with the judges? It was based solely on entertainment alone; no rules basically and was for showtunes and outlawed tunes primarily. Both of these were big hits and soon fiddlers were planning well in advance for them! I think they helped add back an element of fun and camaraderie among contestants that was beginning to be lost. I think the chance to be around other players better than yourself, or maybe just different than yourself is one of the most valuable aspects of contests. I am also thankful that contests allowed me to meet personally the "ideals" I had listened to and learned from. There are few other types of music or outlets for them where you can actually sit with people who have inspired you and have them teach you a new tune for free even. I think there is always room for improvement though. For instance I think contest producers should devote more time to their selection of judges. There is nothing more frustrating for fiddlers than to play before the town barber or banker as opposed to actual, active fiddlers. The tunes and styles can vary so much from region to region, that it is also important to have an equal representation of them in the judges' panel as well.

When I am playing at a contest, I try to stay away from tunes that have been played to death, unless I think I have something particularly new or creative to offer in it. Likewise, playing a very obscure tune is not a good idea as well. I play things like "Durang's Hornpipe," "Leather Britches," "Wild John," "Sally Goodin," "Waggoner" or "Done Gone" for breakdowns. For waltzes, I favor things like "Yellow Rose Waltz," "Chancellor's Waltz," "Taylor's Waltz," "Kentucky Waltz," or "Velvet's Waltz." For tunes of choice, I play things like "Clarinet Polka," "Jesse Polka," "Crafton's Blues," or "Cotton Patch Rag." [In many a contest, a fiddler plays one breakdown, one waltz, and one tune of choice, which may belong to either of those categories, or, more frequently, will explore yet another genre, as exemplified by the tunes Lark cites.]

I think fiddlers are set apart from other Americans much the same way that antique collectors or people who follow vintage cars for instance; we collect old tunes! I suppose that anyone who belongs to a certain group has very adamant feelings about what they are a part of. With fiddling, there is a certain amount of pride in knowing that you are part of a group who is preserving a traditional music. I think fiddling teaches people to be creative, dedicated, and disciplined. Fiddling teaches the value in the preservation of an American artform.

Wes Westmoreland III

The first time I attended the Texas State Fiddle Championship and Fiddlers Frolics, in April of 2000, three men who were obviously good friends sat at the judging table, all three bearing mustaches and two with Stetson hats. The most animated among them was Wes Westmoreland III, a past and future state champion. The competition is just two mornings and afternoons long, and the same judges preside over nearly all of it. And when the judges weren't sitting at their table listening intently to fiddling, they were eating, jamming, or, rarely and briefly, sleeping. It was absolutely clear that no serious interviewing could ever take place during this contest. I finally reached Wes by phone the evening of July 2, 2003.

C: Tell me a little bit about your parents: where they're from, and what they did, and if they fiddled.

W: Let's see, my great-granddad played until he cut his finger off, his left index finger. He's the one that got my Granddad playing. And back in those days, they didn't let the little kids hold the fiddle . . . because fiddles were something special. So that's why you hear about them playing ham cans and stuff like that. When Grandpa was about seventeen or eighteen, he went to sneaking his Dad's fiddle from underneath the bed when Grandpa Winfield was out plowing. And [when the surgeons reattached Grandpa Winfield's finger, it remained] real rigid, so he couldn't really play the fiddle any more. So the way Grandpa learned a lot of stuff was from Grandpa Winfield whistling it to him . . .

Anyway, so my Granddad played, and he's the one that got me started, when I was a little kid . . . I'd go spend my entire summers with him. I was too young to play fiddle then—didn't have one—I didn't *really* start until I was nine. But I was hearing it all the time . . . My Dad plays. My Uncle Gene plays the guitar, and I have a cousin who plays guitar. On Sundays, when we'd all get together for a family thing, we'd eat dinner and watch the Cowboys get beat [the Dallas Cowboys football team, who certainly have had their ups and downs], then we'd go in . . . the kitchen and play the fiddle . . . So my granddad . . . taught me the best he could. Because, the way he had to learn . . . like I said, either from Grandpa Winfield, or . . . they used to have radio shows. I'm sure you've heard about them; from Howdy Forester, and Georgia Slim [Rutland], those radio shows out of Tennessee. He would listen to those, and you'd get to hear a song one time, on a Sunday at noon or whenever it was that they had that radio show, and he had to remember it until the next week. And maybe you got to hear it again; maybe you heard another one. That's how *he* had to learn. It got a little bit easier with me, because I [was learning] at about the time that cassette recorders got pretty popular. I was able to record some stuff and actually get it a little closer [to the originals]. I never paid for a formal lesson . . . I had people show me, or I learned it on my own.

C: Did you have a collection of cassette tapes?

W: I recorded people when they'd let me, at jam sessions. And I'd sit there and play them over and over and over and over again until I got it, or figured out I got close. And then I'd go back to [a fiddler] and say "Hey, how did you exactly do this?" Or maybe I'd just watch them real close. And I did all right until I got up about eighteen and a guy named Bill Gilbert went to showing me, and he reworked my bow arm. There's a difference in Texas fiddle players in their bow arm.

It's something we're pretty proud of, actually. It's something that Major Franklin and Benny Thomasson, Norman and Vernon Soloman, Lewis Franklin, and all these guys that are my heroes did: they kind of innovated it, and we've carried it on past that.

C: Going back a little bit, where did your great-grandfather and grandfather and father live?
W: Comanche County, Texas [70 miles WSW of Fort Worth]. My great-grandpa moved there in . . . either around 1880 or around the 1900s. The family history: we moved across the Mississippi to Leon County [120 miles SES of Dallas]—right around Huntsville—and it was us and the Hillhauses and a few others—so I'm kin to a lot of Hillhauses. My great-grandmother was a Hillhaus. And they moved all the way across to Cloudcroft in [New] Mexico [just East of Alamogorda], and that was too far. So they came back and settled in Comanche County back in the early 1900s. That's where we're based—the Westmorelands—in Comanche County.

C: And what were their professions?
W: Farmers, pretty much. And eventually, Grandpa, when he got up past the [first world] war, he moved out to Lamesa, Texas, which is in West Texas [30 miles south of Lubbock], and drove a truck for a living. That's where my dad and everybody graduated from high school, out there in Lamesa. And then he moved back to Comanche County, where his mom and dad and all his [siblings lived]. My grandpa [was one of] twelve brothers and sisters . . . He was the baby of the family and the only one that played . . . And then we moved back into Comanche County in '75. And that's where we've been based ever since. After that, Grandpa run a front-end loader for the county roads. . . . When I'd spend my summers with him, I'd get up and go to work with him, carrying my BB gun, and I'd hunt lizards all day long. When we got through, we'd go squirrel hunting or fishing or something. When most people were out riding skateboards, or whatever they were doing, I was out doing that with Grandpa.

C: And what was your Dad's profession?
W: Dad [has been] a deputy sheriff in Hamilton County [just east of Comanche County] for maybe thirty years.

C: Do you have students?
W: Not any formal ones. There's . . . a senior in high school now . . . and I'm teaching him some guitar lessons, and mandolin, and I'll give him some fiddle lessons too. I don't have any really formal students. . . . I spent some time with

[Bryan Beken], when I was down around Conroe, [30 miles north of] Houston, going to school. His mama would come down about once a week, and we'd work knee to knee, the way we teach down here. You know: I do, you do. And if you don't do it right, I'll play it to you again. We ear train, we teach by ear. Nothing's written down. And the way I teach—the way I try to teach—is I want you to learn the song, but I want you to learn it *your* way. Does that make sense? In a way, you lose something, but you also gain something. Because it's not going to get any better if you play it the same way that somebody did back in the '30s. So it gets a little better—it changes and it grows—or maybe it doesn't get as good: who knows? But it changes. And it should. If I played everything exactly like Howdy Forester, I would never be any better than Howdy. [In fact,] I would never be as good as Howdy, because nobody's better at [Howdy's style] than Howdy. . . . And that's the way I was trying to teach Bryan. I wanted to show him how to play; then I wanted to show him how to play it different. I'd say: "Now you make it up; you change it a little bit, to make it suit you." And eventually, I'd say, "I want to teach you until you don't need me. I don't want to sit there and depend on you getting every note exactly the way I play it."

C: When you were a kid, what kind of music was in your house besides fiddle music?
W: Fiddle music, pretty much! Mom liked Elvis Presley, of course, back in those days. But there wasn't a whole lot of straight-up country music other than what we heard on the radio. It was pretty much fiddle music, what we listened to.

I listen to tapes I've listened to for the last thirty years. I *still* listen to them. And every now and then I pick something up out of there that I've missed all these years. And I try to learn it thataway. . . .

When you say: "What kind of music was in my house?" . . . I listened to a whole lot of Bob Wills and western swing stuff. That's a big influence on what I do, a huge influence. And when I was real young, when I first started playing, not only was I playing breakdowns, and fiddle things like that, but I was also playing dances for the senior citizens. When I was fifteen, and playing in party houses where I probably had no business being in . . . I was playing dances, sometimes with my Grandpa, sometimes with some other friends. I was usually by far the baby of whatever bunch was playing together. But because of that, I learned a bunch of things that a lot of kids don't learn, those little things like "Put Your Little Foot" and what they call a "Paul Jones." And those kinds of things I still know how to do because I'd played them as a kid for those old folks. And a Charleston! I'll tell you something real funny: I used to play a senior citizen's dance there in Angelina County, and they'd have a Charleston contest. And what it'd amount to: I'd play a rag, like "Cotton Patch Rag" or "Beaumont Rag" or something like that, and all those old-timers in there would Charleston. And they'd Charleston until somebody won, however they'd decide to do it. There was a little—I was about fifteen, and didn't pay much attention—there was always a little man there, that could really dance really good. And he was about 105 pounds wet, and probably about eighty years old, with one lung. And I would play, and that poor old man would go to pumpin', and Grandpa'd lean over, and he'd say "Son, you'd better wind that tune up before you kill that man!" I tell you what, that old devil never quit dancing until I was done.

I played a whole lot of dances, a lot of Ray Price and Durham McCall and those old full-force western swing and shuffle things. I learned "The Key Is in the Mailbox," "Please Release Me," and those things I grew up on too, along with a lot of western swing, a lot of Bob Wills. That's one of my big influences, big heroes. And the fiddle players like Jesse Ashlock and Joe Holly and Tommy Canfield, and of course Johnny Gimble and Keith Coleman and those guys are all my heroes. I listen to them a lot. So really I've had about three or four complete different areas of influences on what I play, on what I've tried to learn from. One of them's western swing stuff from Gimble and those guys; J. R. Chatwell, maybe some guys you don't know about. There's also the jazz people like Joe Venuti, Stéphane Grappelli, and Sven Asmussen and a few of those other ones that I can't recall off the top of my head . . . And Eddie South is probably one that you never heard of. Hunt up Eddie South: he's really good. He'll surprise you. And of course I had my breakdown heroes, Benny Thomasson and the others I named off. And then I got off into some classical stuff. I can't do it, but I admire it, like Itzhak Perlman and those guys. And I listen to a lot of that. And then there's also stuff that's not fiddling, like the big band stuff. I like the trios, the Benny Goodman Trios, Quartets, Quintets, those kinds of things. Clarinet players; I've stolen a lot from clarinet players, I'll put it that way. They play some really cool stuff.

C: So have you just described your collection of recordings?
W: You wouldn't believe what I've got over here. I've got stuff that sounds like it's from India, some of it sounds like it's from Jamaica, violinists playing . . . I've got an Itzhak Perlman tape playing klezmer music . . . there's some pretty cool things in there. I'll glean a few things out of there . . . and that's just fiddle playing stuff. I've got rock 'n' roll and folk and stuff mixed in there too. I'm a pretty big Beatles fan. I like James Taylor and Paul Simon and those guys. They've got some pretty neat guitar chords that they do that tickles me. So anyway, I've got a pretty wide range [of influences], and I think a lot of fiddle players do . . . You listen to all this *other* stuff and you're *playing* "Sally Goodin!"

C: A lot of stuff sneaks into "Sally Goodin."
W: Oh yeah. But you know what—have you ever heard that old 78 of Eck Robertson playing that?

C: Yeah!
W: Can you believe that guy was that good back in those days? Did you know that that's cross-keyed? His whole fiddle is ringing. It's just him by himself. It's EAEA he's got it tuned. And he also, playing by himself, he speeds up, slows down, speeds up—it's just him—but the way he does it sounds fabulous! I heard that again the other day, and I was just amazed as how good it sounded.

C: He was an amazing guy.
W: Yes he was. I actually got to meet him a little bit before he died. He lived to be ninety-something. I've got some pictures of him somewhere, [from] when I was a little kid. When I was a kid, I didn't realize what I was seeing back then. But I do get to remember him. I remember Major Franklin a little bit. He'd pretty much quit by the time I got to be old enough to know what was going on. But I got to meet a few people that's pretty cool.

C: You mentioned earlier that you'd played a lot of dances when you were a kid. Do you still do that at all?
W: Oh, yeah. I played a job the other night. I played for a family reunion in Palo Pinto County, Texas [30 miles east of Fort Worth]. Beautiful: right on the Brazos River. A guy named Smith built a house on a bluff overlooking the Brazos River. You can see two miles either way. It's one of the most pretty places I've ever seen. But we played a little trio. Dick Gimble (Johnny Gimble's son) played a guitar, Buck Reems sang and played guitar, and I played fiddle. And we played stuff like "Big Butter and Egg Man"—you know that thing Merle Haggard cut. We did Merle Haggard songs and George Strait songs and a whole lot of Bob Wills, a couple of James Taylor songs, just whatever they wanted to hear. I played a bunch of normal fiddle dance things, like "Jesse Polka" and "Cotton-Eyed Joe" and those things.

C: So if you were to have a typical week—and I know nobody does—but if you had an average week, how many hours would you be devoting to doing what on the fiddle?
W: I go two, three weeks and not even pick it up. But then I go play a job . . . And it was really like that when I was a kid. I never really formally sit down and say "I'm going to practice a couple hours" . . . But what I did do was play a lot.

We'd go to fiddle contests every weekend somewhere, and I might play three, four, five hours at them, at jam sessions. And *that* was my practice. Now I did do some learning, and sit around trying to figure out things when I was young, but I would do it to figure out something: I wouldn't sit there and do it to practice.

C: Well, I was talking to Carl [Hopkins] the other day, and he told a story about you guys driving around in a pickup truck and listening to tapes.
W: Oh, yeah! And arguing: we'll play "Who's This Playing?" like "Guess the Fiddler." And if you don't do good, you get razzed real bad. Carl and I are real good at it. I mean, in about three notes, we know who it is . . . In lieu of practice, that's what I do: I listen to it constantly. . . . Right now, there's a fiddle tape in my car, and when I go from here to the hospital, I listen to fiddling all the way up there and all the way back. . . . I hardly ever listen to the radio; I'd rather listen to a fiddle tape of some sort. You know what one of them big old boxes looks like. I've got about two or three of those boxes just level full with loose cassette tapes. I go through them . . . I know my good ones. I have them labeled, and I have some really good ones, but then I have a bunch in there I don't even know what's on them.

C: Of the different sorts of tunes that you play today, do you prefer breakdowns over waltzes or stuff like that?
W: As I get older, I like waltzes better. When I was a kid, I couldn't stand them. It's all about testosterone . . . the older I get, also, I've learned a lot about harmony. I like playing some really nice harmony parts now. I think that's a lot of fun, and especially fun because there's not a whole lot of people can do it. It's one thing to play the first part harmony of something. It's another thing to figure out the second part, and the third part. Actually the way you should say it is first, third, and fifth, and then another part after that, even. That fifth part don't sound like anything worthwhile [played separately]. If you play it [alone] you think: "That's horrible." But when you put it all together and mix it all together, it's really pretty. And I learned a lot how to do that . . . when I was playing with Mel Tillis. When I first went to work for him, there was three fiddle players, and I had to play the fifth part. So I had to learn that. And Randy Elmore told me this: "While you're here, at the same time [as you learn the fifth] you learn the lead and the second, too, because you never know. And sure enough . . . within three weeks, I've gone from fifth to playing the lead, and having to teach a new guy how to play the third, the part I've been playing [immediately before]. So that was kind of crazy. . . .

That was nine months of the year, two shows a day, six days a week, for ten years, in Branson, Missouri. And before that, when I was in college the first time around, I played a lot with Red Stegall, and some with Moe Bandy, and a few of those guys. . . . That's how I made money going through school, between that and fiddle contests, and dances I'd played . . . And the same thing when I was in school this last time up there in Houston. When everybody else was putting in tech work at a pharmacy, working for a few bucks an hour, I was off someplace playing a fiddle dance making about two or three times what they was making. That's how I made my money, plus I had a lot of fun doing it. So I played like the barbecue cook-off we have here, the Houston Rodeo, and things like that. . . . If you're asking if I ever quit playing: nah, I'll never quit playing. This is not even really a hobby, it's just *fun*. And working a fiddle job, you make some money, but the ones I work now, I work because the people are fun. And I love it, I just love playing.

C: Well, you've worked with so many fiddlers and known so many—is there anything like a character profile? What are fiddlers like, as opposed to the general population, would you say?
W: Fiddle players are a different bunch—I'm sure you've figured that out by now—a little different breed. . . . I don't know if you could really characterize us. We're fun; everybody's different. We have some pretty sedate ones, and we have some ones that you think: "Oh, my God, I could never tell anybody what you just did."

C: Well, one thing that most people have said is that there's usually a pretty powerful sense of humor.
W: If you don't have it, you can't survive. Because for one thing, the other fiddle players would never let you up for air. . . . And another thing—you know, you're playing these fiddle contests, and you know, you try to deny it, but everybody has an ego about it. And you just get completely creamed in a contest, and it hurts. So you get your feelings hurt, but the thing is, the way you look at it is: there's no fiddle contest ever, and ever will be, that's a really true test of what kind of fiddle player you are. You know what the biggest, best, true test is of that? If you can sit down in a jam session and play two hours, with all your peers around you hollering at you. For two hours, and entertain, and never play the same song twice . . . you look around, and you're ten-twelve-twenty people deep in a circle. That's a fiddle player. . . . A fiddle player gets out there in the pickups, or out around somebody's motor home, or out around the back end of a contest, and he and two or three guitar players get together and go to playing, and directly they've got twenty people deep all around him. . . . Carl [Hopkins] may not ever win all the big contests, but he's a *fiddle player*. Because when he goes to playing every-

body else huddles up around him because it's a show. He's fixing to entertain. . . . It may not be the most perfect, but it's the most heartfelt. It's got the most soul. And he can sit there and play . . . three days and never play the same song twice. He knows so much. He knows so many songs and has been around so long, and he has his own way of playing: he don't sound like nobody else. And that is a fiddle player. When I first met Bryan Beken, I told his mother; this is the deal I made: "I'll teach your boy however you want me to teach him. But if you want me to teach him how to play in a fiddle contest . . . Here's the two ways you can go. I can teach him how to play in a fiddle contest and win it. Or I can teach him to be that over there." And I pointed over at Carl, and just like I said, there's about eight people deep all the way around him, he was playing, and laughing, and hollering, and having the best time.

C: What are the most valuable aspects of contests? What's a contest good for?
W: You know what the best thing is for them? You're able to make a few bucks and get to see everybody. It's a good excuse to get together in someplace called Crockett or Nacogdoches and have a jam session. That's essentially what they are. I mean, you go and try to win them—I'll be the last one to tell you you don't go and try to win them—but, really and truly, the fun part of it is the night before, in somebody's motel room, or outside by the pickups or something. That's where all the fun takes place. The contest is just something you've got to go through, in a way. I don't mean to demean it, like it sounds like I'm doing, because it is

Figure 17. Wes Westmoreland III competing at the Texas State Championship in 2004, in the Hallettsville Knights of Columbus Hall.

important, and it does help promote [fiddling], and it keeps it going. Without the fiddle contest, somebody from Fort Worth might not ever see somebody from Houston . . . But with these fiddle contests, you've got one in Nacogdoches, you've got one in Burleson, you've got one in Dallas, you have one in Hallettsville that you went to, and everybody knows: we'll meet there, and we'll play in the fiddle contest, and we'll sit around all night and play and pick, and pick at each other. And it's almost like a . . . oh . . . how can I say it? We're kind of clannish. We've got a group . . . well, put it like this: How many high school people do you know that you still keep up with? People you grew up with and went to high school with? Our fiddler bunch—I've known these guys since I was nine, and we're still best friends. And I'm not just talking about one or two people; I'm talking about twenty, twenty-five, thirty people, or more, and their families. And their sons or grandsons that are now coming up playing fiddles . . . And we don't just talk every once in a while, we see each other a lot. It's like a bond that stretches out past the fact that you graduated from the same high school.

C: A lot of people use the word "family," but I don't know if that's quite the right one.
W: It's probably more like a family, but it's a little stronger than that even, be-cause there's family members that you don't care too much for, but fiddle players hang together really tight. And we respect each other. And we have the same interests in a lot of ways. It's really pretty cool. I got to thinking about that the other day: people that I met when I was nine years old, I'm still best friends with. And old guys too. Old, young, it doesn't matter, it crosses the generations.

C: Yeah, and I don't know much else that does that.
W: That's right. That's *right*. This really crosses the generations. And my best heroes—most of them are dead now . . . And I can appreciate somebody eighty years old that plays as good as he can play . . . And that's something else that I try to teach those kids: I don't care how you play or what you play . . . you never pooh-pooh somebody's playing. Something he does is better than anybody else. And, from what people will call a scratcher, I've learned some pretty good licks. . . .
     I don't know if you've ever seen one of them 45 rpm records that Shorty put out [Jim Chancellor, known as "Texas Shorty"]. They're little 45s that he put out back when he was sixteen, seventeen, eighteen years old, back in the late '50s. . . . When I was a little kid, my granddad had a bunch of them, and I nailed them. In fact, I've still got them, and I still listen to them. And I would take those 45 rpm little records, and put them on my record player, and slow them down to 33, and tune my fiddle down to them, and sit there—this was when I was nine,

ten, twelve, fourteen years old—and worry, and cry, and be mad and frustrated because I couldn't make it sound like Shorty did. I didn't know why. I would hit that wall, and I would hit that wall, and six months later I would [realize] that's it! That's what he did! So I spent those times being mad and frustrated—can't get over the hump—and some of it was [that] I wasn't playing it the way that it was, and some of it was just pure maturity, maturing into your fiddle playing.... Anyway, I've walked every step everybody else has about learning, so I can identify with them, and if somebody messes up: been there. Nobody can mess up as bad as I have in a fiddle contest!

C: Well, you've done all right lately!
W: I've learned to cover up some! I messed up in Hallettsville [where he once again won the state championship in 2003] ... I played a fiddle contest one time, and my bow slipped. I didn't lose the grip, but it flipped sideways, and the fiddle bow hair went in and around my fine tuners. And I just had to stop, and say "Excuse me," and unwrap it from my fine tuners, and then go back to playing. I was mortified. I've had big bluebottle flies hit me right in the eye; things crawling all over the back of your neck, and I've had storms blow in right in the middle of a tune. We were playing in Gustine one time, and one of those blue northers blew in. Right in the middle of "Billy in the Low Ground," the wind picked up to about thirty miles an hour, and it started trying to rain, and I'm trying to finish this stinking tune, and I wouldn't quit, because I thought it was kind of funny....

C: If contests were to be changed at all, how should they be changed?
W: That's a pretty good question, actually. That's like a night's worth of talking, right there. My ideal contest ... Here's the deal: everybody goes, and they want to play, and you cannot deny them [the chance] to play. They drove 150 miles, 300 miles, across the state of Texas, or from no telling where. We had a lot of people from Idaho come down to the contest in Hallettsville this year, you know. That's a long ways. Well, ideally ... you get three good, knowledgeable fiddle players down there [to judge] that knows how to play, and knows what it's about, understands that it's more than just sounding "good:" that it's heart, soul, there's some difficulty involved, that you can't really judge if you've never really tried to do it. And bear in mind that it's art you're judging; it's not a foot race.... And Hallettsville's one of the better ones at doing this, if not the best one. You pare it down to your top [contestants], and you make them play. You don't just judge it on a couple of tunes; otherwise, people will just learn five, six, seven tunes, and never learn anything else. And really and truly, Hallettsville ought to play us more, ought to play us ten songs apiece, but then that would get too long. I can

understand that: there's time constraints. But to have a real good judged fiddle contest, you make these guys play, and play different kinds of tunes, and not just breakdowns and not just waltzes. You get a broad scope of what a guy can do. Hallettsville's about the best at doing that. At the round robin [the final play-off between the three highest-scoring fiddlers], you'll remember we played a waltz, a rag, a polka, a breakdown, and a swing tune. That's a pretty broad range of tunes, isn't it? You played them one behind the other; you never got to leave the stage. You had to sit right there and listen to the guy in front of you just tear one up. And you had to go in behind him and play it yourself. That's about as good an example of [a contest] as you can have.

C: So, what else, to make that perfect contest?

W: If you judge with five people [as has been done many years at Weiser, and recently at Hallettsville], and you go just on raw scores, you're trying to measure art with a ruler . . . To me, the perfect contest is you get three good judges, and you get a *consensus* of opinion. They confer, they say, "I think this," and "I think that," and if they differ, then you say: "Let's call [the fiddlers] back, and play them off again, and see what you think this time." And you make them play again. And if nobody steps forward and has a clear win, play them off again. And eventually, the fiddle player will shine, and the other one will fall. And it may be that they're both fiddle players, but that day, one guy'll be stronger. And that happens a lot. That's my favorite [scenario], but people judge it with five judges just because it's easier: you judge it with scores, drop out the high and low, take the average of what's left, and you don't have any play-offs, and your contest don't go too long. That's what they're doing at Hallettsville now, and I understand the reason why. But, to me, I like having three and knowing that somebody like Larry Franklin and Dale Morris and Ricky Turpin are the three that was this year . . . it was their opinion, their general consensus that I was the best fiddle player that day. That means more to me than the fact that I got more points than somebody.

[At this point, we went off the record for some time, then returned during a discussion of the format of the "national" contest in Weiser, Idaho, a weeklong affair that is nevertheless so crowded that contestants play abbreviated forms of three tunes during a total of either four or five minutes, depending on the competition bracket and the round of competition.]

W: You know what that's caused? That's caused a lot of new kids to learn, let's see, four rounds? Three rounds times three songs? They learn nine songs. They learn three waltzes a minute long. You show me a "Kelly Waltz" that you can play it in a minute and play it right! Everybody's truncated their tunes because of this contest. And they'll take those tunes and play them [in] all the rest of the contests the rest of the year the same length—[even though there's] no time limit, the same length. But that's how they learn them. They learn them note by note, to fit in that four minutes, and that's how they play them the whole year. And that's wrong. And that's detrimental to fiddle playing. When you play a fiddle song, you play it until you're done with it. If it's two minutes, fine. If it's five minutes, that's what you felt, that's what you play. That's something Texas will never do. There'll never be a time limit in Texas, I guarantee you. . . . Personally, I judge more not so much on "preciseness" as I do soul, what I call singing your song . . . like what they talk about Hank Williams: you could sing a song, but could you make somebody *feel* what you're singing?

C: And what musical elements contribute the most to that, do you think?
W: Part of it is not learning tunes note by note. You learn the *point* of the tune, not the notes. You learn "*Dusty Miller*," you don't learn just the notes of "Dusty Miller." That way, every time you play "Dusty Miller," it's a little bit different, but it's what you feel . . .

C: What are your favorite tunes to play at contests?
W: Well, see, that's just it. You learn that there are some tunes that are stronger, so I'll play "Dusty Miller" and "Tom and Jerry" and "Grey Eagle" and "Sally Johnson" and those breakdowns like that because they're good, strong tunes, they're good strong breakdowns, and you know they'll score well. But if I had my druthers, I'd play some "Waynesboro Reel" or "Butterfly Hornpipe" or some of them other eclectic . . . or "Forked Deer" or one of those like that that nobody plays much at contests any more: I'd just as soon play those. I *do* every now and then . . .

C: What makes the strong tunes strong?
W: I don't know . . . some of it is just it's been done for so long that they accept them as that, and some of it is just that [for example] "Sally Johnson" is just . . . a good melody, it's got a lot of good separate parts in it [and] there's a lot of drive in "Sally Johnson," where there's not in some of these other songs. You know, "Whistlin' Rufus" is a good song, but it's not a driving song, it's not going to grab anybody's attention. You're not going to impress anybody with it. But my problem with the kids is, they're learning "Sally Johnson;" they're not learning "Whistlin' Rufus." And, to me, learning those songs is what a fiddle player is. A fiddle player plays everything, all of them. They learn a song just because it's the song. They don't learn a song [just] to win something with it. . . .

C: You're kind of working around to a question that a lot of fiddlers don't like, and that's: What values do you think fiddling supports?

W: That's difficult, because really there's no redemption to it. And fiddlers can be a pretty sorry lot. And a lot of them get together—and I've been just as bad—and get [very drunk], play, and have fun. No redeeming qualities to it, other than the fact that it's been carried on for generations . . .

C: But on the other hand, you talk about paying homage to these fiddlers.

W: There's a respect. Hey, those guys were before you. And you're learning on top of what they made up. They made the tracks that you're making *already*, and they made it up with no help . . . And they made it, and changed it, and made it as good as they could make it . . . As far as redeeming qualities, you know it's something that's been going on for years, and you don't want it to die down. And it comes and goes. We went through a part in the '80s where we had a fiddle contest every weekend, two or three every weekend. And now it's slowed down; there's not that many right now. But we've got a lot of kids running [around] the place, so it'll come back around again. . . .

Bibliography

"Aged Fiddlers." 1929. *The Etude*, February, 133.

Bailey, Marcus. 1983. "Early Alabama Fiddling." *The Devil's Box* 17:21.

Bayard, Samuel Preston. 1944. *Hill Country Tunes: Instrumental Folk Music of Western Pennsylvania*. Philadelphia: American Folklore Society.

———. 1982. *Dance to the Fiddle, March to the Fife: Instrumental Folk Tunes in Pennsylvania*. University Park: Pennsylvania State University Press.

Behlmer, George K. 2000. "Introduction." Pp. 1–10 in George K. Behlmer and Fred M. Leventhal, eds., *Singular Continuities: Tradition, Nostalgia, and Identity in Modern British Culture*. Stanford, Calif.: Stanford University Press.

Boym, Svetlana. 2001. *The Future of Nostalgia*. New York: Basic Books.

Bronner, Simon J. 1977. "'I Kicked Three Slats Out of My Cradle the First Time I Heard That:' Ken Kane, Country Musician, and American Folklife." *New York Folklore Quarterly* 3 (1–4): 53–81.

Burman-Hall, Linda C. 1975. "Southern American Folk Fiddle Styles." *Ethnomusicology* 19:47–65.

———. 1984. "American Traditional Fiddling: Performance Context and Techniques." In *Performance Practice: Ethnomusicological Perspectives,* edited by Gerard Bèhague. Westport, Conn.: Greenwood.

Burrison, John A. 1977. "Fiddlers in the Alley: Atlanta as an Early Country Music Center." *The Atlanta Historical Bulletin* 21/2:59–87.

Cashman, Ray. 2006. "Critical Nostalgia and Material Culture in Northern Ireland." *Journal of American Folklore* 119 (472): 137–60.

Cauthen, Joyce H. 1989. *With Fiddle and Well-Rosined Bow: Old-Time Fiddling in Alabama*. Tuscaloosa: The University of Alabama Press.

Cohen, Anne, and Norman Cohen. 1977. "Folk and Hillbilly Music: Further Thoughts on Their Relation." *John Edwards Memorial Foundation Quarterly* 13 (46): 50–57.

Cohen, Norman. 1975. "Clayton McMichen: His Life and Music." *John Edwards Memorial Foundation Quarterly* 11/3:117–23.

Combs, Josiah H. 1960. "The Highlander's Music." *Kentucky Folklore Record* 6 (4): 108–22.

Daniel, Wayne W. 1980. "The Georgia Old-Time Fiddlers' Convention: 1920 Edition." *John Edwards Memorial Foundation Quarterly* 16 (58): 67–73.

Dulles, Foster Rhea. 1965. *A History of Recreation*. 2d ed. New York: Appleton-Century Crofts.

Dunnavant, Robert, Jr. 1995. *Historic Limestone County, Alabama*. 2d ed. Athens, Ala.: Pea Ridge Press.

Ellison, Ralph. 1968. "The Golden Age, Time Past." In *Shadow and Act*. New York: Random House.

Falassi, Alejandro. 1987. *Time Out of Time: Essays on the Festival*. Albuquerque: University of New Mexico Press.

"Fiddling to Henry Ford." 1926. *Literary Digest* 88 (1): 33–38.

Fischer, Carl, Inc. 1894. *Carl Fischer's New and Revised Edition of Celebrated Tutors: Excelsior Method for the Fife*. Rev. ed. New York: Fischer.

Goertzen, Chris. 1982. "Philander Seward's 'Musical Deposit' and the History of American Instrumental Folk Music." *Ethnomusicology* 26 (1): 1–10.

———. 1991. "Mrs. Joe Person's Popular Airs: Early Blackface Minstrel Tunes in Oral Tradition." *Ethnomusicology* 35 (1): 31–53.

———. 1996. "Balancing Local and National Fiddle Styles at American Fiddle Contests." *American Music* 14 (3): 352–81.

———. 2004. "George Cecil McLeod, Mississippi's Fiddling Senator, and the Modern History of American Fiddling." *American Music* 22 (3): 339–79.

Goertzen, Chris, and Alan Jabbour. 1987. "George P. Knauff's Virginia Reels and Fiddling in the Antebellum South." *American Music* 5 (2): 121–44.

Gow, Niel. [1792]. *A Third Collection of Strathspey Reels &c for the Piano-Forte, Violin, and Violoncello. Dedicated to the Most Noble the Marchioness of Tweeddale*. Edinburgh: author.

Graf, Sharon Poulson. 1999. "Traditionalization at the National Oldtime Fiddlers' Contest: Politics, Power, and Authenticity." Diss., Michigan State University.

Graham, Philip. 1951. *Showboats: The History of an American Institution*. Austin: University of Texas Press.

Guthrie, Charles S. 1972. "Whitey Stearnes: Troubadour of the Cumberland Valley." *Kentucky Folklore Record* 18 (2): 52–55.

Hamm, Charles. 1983. *Yesterdays: Popular Song in America*. New York: Norton.

Howe, Elias. 1843. *The Musician's Companion*. 3 vols. Boston: author.

———. 1864. *Musician's Omnibus*. Boston: author.

Jabbour, Alan. 1977. "American Fiddle Tunes from the Archive of Folk Song." Notes to one 33⅓ rpm disc, Library of Congress AFS L62.

Knauff, George P. 1839. *Virginia Reels*. 4 vols. Baltimore: Willig.

Koon, William Henry. 1969. "The Country Professional: Record Reviews." *Tennessee Folklore Society Bulletin* 35 (2): 56–61.

Library of Congress, Music Division. 1942. *Checklist of Recorded Songs in the English Language in the Archive of American Folk Song to July, 1940*. Washington, D.C.: Library of Congress.

Lincecum, Dr. Gideon. 1874. "Personal Reminiscences of an Octogenarian." *The American Sportsman* (21 November).

Lincecum, Jerry Bryan, and Edward Hake Phillips, eds. 1994. *Adventures of a Frontier Naturalist: The Life and Times of Dr. Gideon Lincecum*. College Station: Texas A&M University Press.

Malone, Bill C. 1968. *Country Music U.S.A.* Austin: University of Texas Press for the American Folklore Society.

Meade, Guthrie T., Jr. 1969. "From the Archives: 1914 Atlanta Fiddle Convention." *John Edwards Memorial Foundation Quarterly* 5 (1–13): 27–30.

One Thousand Fiddle Tunes. 1940. Chicago: M. M. Cole.

Pepper, J. W. 1896. *The Mammoth Collection of Popular and Standard Music for the Violin*. 1893. Enlarged reprint, Philadelphia and Chicago: Pepper.

Person, Mrs. Joe [Alice Morgan Person]. 1889. *A Collection of Popular Airs as Arranged and Played Only by Mrs. Joe Person at the Southern Expositions.* Richmond, Va.: Hume and Minor.

Randolph, Vance. 1932. *Ozark Mountain Folks.* New York: Vanguard Press.

Ryan, William. 1883. *Ryan'a Mammoth Collection. 1050 Reels and Jigs, Hornpipes, Clogs, Walk-Arounds, Essences, Strathspeys, Highland Flings, and Contra Dances.* Boston: Howe.

Starobinski, Jean. 1966. "The Idea of Nostalgia." Trans. William S. Kemp. *Diogenes* 54:81–103.

Stoutamire, Albert. 1972. Music *of the Old South: Colony to Confederacy.* Madison, Wis.: Fairleigh Dickinson University Press.

Titon, Jeff Todd. 2001. *Old-Time Kentucky Fiddle Tunes.* Lexington: University Press of Kentucky.

Webster's Third International Dictionary of the English Language. 1971. Springfield, Mass.: G. & C. Merriam Co.

Wells, Paul F. 1976. "Mellie Dunham: Maine's Champion Fiddler." *John Edwards Memorial Foundation Quarterly* 12 (43): 112–18.

Wilgus, Donald K. 1971. "Introduction" [to an issue devoted to the study of commercialized folk music, especially hillbilly music]. *Western Folklore* 30 (3): 171–76.

Wolfe, Charles K. 1977. "New Light on the Early Opry: Dr. Bate's Letters." *John Edwards Memorial Foundation Quarterly* 13 (45): 1–3.

———. 1978. "Columbia Records and Old-Time Music." *John Edwards Memorial Foundation Quarterly* 14 (51): 118–44.

———. 1980. "An 1899 Fiddlers' Carnival." *The Devil's Box* 14 (4): 50–52.

Young, Henry. 1971. "Narmour and Smith—A Brief Biography." *John Edwards Memorial Foundation Quarterly* 7 (1/21): 31–34.

Index

34, 44, 48, 55–60, 85–87, 117, 120, 138, 146;
inebriation and, 86–87, 90, 152; jamming
at, 3, 30, 41–42, 44, 47–49, 81, 87, 124, 127,
138, 146–47; judges and judging, 29–30, 33,
40–41, 46, 83, 111, 113–17, 138–39, 149–50;
race at, 62; scholarships financed by fiddle
contests, 30, 53, 109
fiddle tunes: characters of, 78, 101, 112;
collections of, 9, 13; and religion, 11,
52–53, 62; repertoires, 23, 79; Scottish, 7,
93–94; structures of, 92–105; titles of, 93;
transmission of, 24
fiddlers: African American, 7–8, 14, 63, 75,
106–7; associations, 9; gender of, 89–90,
111–12, 135–36; Native American, 63;
New England, 9; personalities of, 5, 124,
126; primitive, 10; professions of, 69–70;
spanning generations, 10–12, 15, 18, 22,
54–55, 63–64, 66, 68–69, 88, 111–12, 127,
134, 140, 148, 152; urban revivalists, 39, 48,
62, 63, 65, 73, 76, 86, 89, 112–13, 119, 127
Fiddler's Grove Ole Time Fiddler's and
Bluegrass Festival, 52–53
fiddling: by families, 15, 25, 31, 37, 67–68, 88,
108, 140; fashionable, 5; learning to fiddle,
9–12, 16, 24, 70–73, 127, 128, 130, 140, 145,
148, 151; moral qualities of, 19, 80–91;
old-time, 4, 22–24; at political gatherings,
12, 16–18; on radio, 12–13, 16–17, 19, 23;
regional styles, 41–42, 46, 65–66, 78–80,
92–120; school programs, 18; sinful, 5, 10; at
state fairs, 25, 27–30; subculture associated
with, 8, 14, 22–23, 25, 27, 29, 49, 113, 134;
tape recording(s) of, 16, 140–42, 145;
teaching of, 44, 74–75, 77, 124–25, 132–33,
141–42; techniques, 23, 39, 42, 113, 128,
131–33, 140, 144–45; variation techniques,
40, 78–80, 96–97, 101–5, 114, 117, 150–51
Fischer, Carl, 8
"Fisher's Hornpipe," 8, 13
flatfoot dancing. *See* buck dancing
Flatt and Scruggs, 137
Flippen, Benton, 122
"Flowers of Edinburgh," 8
Flying Jenny, 113
Fodor, Eugene, 74

folk music revivals, viii, 8–9, 13, 16
Ford, Henry, 11, 13
Forester, Howdy, 142
"Forked Deer," 151
"Fox Chase," 13
Franklin, Larry, 150
Franklin, Lewis, 141
Franklin, Major, 74, 141, 144
Fraser, Alisdair, 74
Fries, Virginia, fiddle contest in, 34, 53, 89
Fruitdale, Alabama, 23
Fulcher, Lee, 22, 25

Galax, Virginia, and fiddle contest in, 14,
34–38, 41–42, 47–48, 52, 82, 89, 112, 117,
121, 132
"Galveston Flood," 111
Gary Lewis and the Playboys, 28
"General Harrison's March," 7
Georgia Old Time Fiddlers Association, 9
Gimble, Dick, 144
Gimble, Johnny, 143–44
Goertzen, Ellen, 33
Goertzen, Kate, 33
"Golden Slippers," 107
good old days. *See* nostalgia
Goodman, Benny, 74, 143
Goolsby, Jim, 10
gospel tunes, 22, 54, 78, 111, 136
Gow, Niel, 93–94
Grand Ole Opry, 19
Grappelli, Stéphane, 74, 143
Grayson and Whitter, 72
Great Britain, 5
Greene County, Mississippi, 17–18, 20–22
"Grey Eagle," 113, 151
Griffin, M. L., 15
Grim, Brian, 66, 70–71, 76, 79, 86, 88, 94, 97
guitar, 20, 22, 25, 44, 110, 112
Gulf Coast of Mississippi, 15
"Gypsy Davie," 111

Hafer, Johannes, 61
Haggard, Merle, 144
"Hail Columbia," 7
Haley, Ed, 131–32

Walnut Hill Old-Time Band, 32

waltzes, 4, 45, 55, 77–79, 88, 112–13, 119, 137, 139, 145, 150

"Washington's Grand March," 7

"Waynesboro Reel," 151

Weddle, Ivan, 122

Weiser, Idaho, fiddle contest in, 14, 38–43, 45, 47–48, 57–58, 68, 75, 87, 103, 114, 150

West Jefferson, North Carolina. *See* Ashe County Old Time Fiddler's and Bluegrass Convention

Westmoreland, Wes, III, 56, 67, 70, 72, 77, 83, 87, 90, 102–5, 112, 139–52

"When the Wagon was New," 111

"Whiskey Before Breakfast," 56

"Whistler's Waltz," 39

"Whistlin' Rufus," 151

Whittinghill, Joel, 67, 70, 74, 78, 114, 116, 119

"Who Comes In When I Go Out?," 56

"Wild John," 139

Willig, George, Jr., 100n

Wills, Bob, 142–44

Wilson, Keith, 40

Wine, Melvin, 68

Winner, Septimus, 8

Wolfe, Charles, 12–13

"Yellow Rose Waltz," 139

Yesterdays, 61

"Zip Coon," 5

Zukerman, Pinchas, 74

Zwinger, Theodor, 118